3/12/88

To Fred

From biplanes
to the stars
What a beautiful
flight path you
have set.

Tom Simmons

# The Brown Condor

# The *Brown Condor*

## The True Adventures of John C. Robinson

### Thomas E. Simmons

**Bartleby Press**

Silver Spring, Maryland

Printed in the United States of America

Published and Distributed by:

Bartleby Press
11141 Georgia Avenue
Suite A-6
Silver Spring, Maryland 20902

**Library of Congress Cataloging-in-Publication Data**

Simmons, Thomas E., 1936-
   The brown condor.

   1. Robinson, John C.   2. Air pilots—United States—Biography.
3. Air pilots—Ethiopia—Biography.   I. Title
TL540.R57S56   1988      629.13′092′4 [B]       87-22948
ISBN 0-910155-09-7

To
Kay, Scott and Jack
who understand

# Acknowledgements

The following deserve thanks for their suggestions, encouragement and contributions: Curtis Graves, for his outstanding help in research and interviews, Dr. Jerry Brown, Edgar Beauchamp, Jack Howell, Al Key, Bertha Robinson Stokes, Miomi Godine, Cornelius Coffey, Harold Hurd, Janet Waterford Bragg, Inniss Ford, Yosef Ford, my editor, Donnali Shor and others too numerous to mention.

I would also like to acknowledge the assistance of the following research facilities and organizations: National Archives, Library of Congress, Tuskegee University Library and the research archives of the *Sun-Herald*.

# Contents

# Foreword

Publications like Alex Haley's *Roots* demonstrated the potential of imaginative literature in addressing important themes in Afro-American history. It was discovered with renewed appreciation that techniques employed in the historical novel could illuminate the past, in particular those regions of the historical landscape that were shrouded in relative darkness. For the story of black Americans, such an approach possessed appeal: the historical literature dealing with the black experience was meager and the surviving primary materials needed to write conventional histories were often lacking.

The participation of blacks in aviation mirrors this larger historical problem. The airplane has transformed modern life, and black Americans, alive to the adventure of flight and its career opportunities, have from the beginning endeavored to gain entrance to the aeronautical community at all levels. The prevailing social mores of American life in the first half of the 20th century, however, either mandated or encouraged racial segregation in most areas of modern technology. Aeronautics was no different: for many years flying was deemed off limits to blacks. There was even a pervasive attitude on the part of the predominantly white aeronautical world that blacks lacked the aptitude to fly.

In the 1920s, only a very few blacks managed to obtain licenses to fly and to do so they had to overcome the extraordinary barriers of racial segregation. Learning to fly, however, was only the first step. Once you obtained your license there were many frustrations along the way: the managers of smaller airports were frequently hostile to black fliers even to the point of refusing services and fuel.

John C. Robinson belonged to this pioneering generation of black pilots and knew firsthand the difficulties of breaking into aviation.

Although few records survive to tell his story, Thomas Simmons has taken the essentials of Robinson's life story and recast them into the framework of a historical novel. A biography emerges, one that blends the historical data with an imaginative retelling of Robinson's life. To add authenticity, Simmons systematically examined Robinson's life, by interviewing people who knew him, and reconstructing the historical nuances of place and time. The result is an effective one: Robinson emerges in these pages as a bold and talented pilot who flew both in America and Africa at various times of his life.

Robinson's years of flying covered three decades, beginning in the late 1920s and extending into the 1950s. During this time, the climate for blacks in aviation began to change, subtly at first, and then radically.

The paradox of John Robinson's career is that he would not benefit personally from the changes in the American aviation community that allowed, if reluctantly at first, greater black involvement. Ironically, John Robinson, a man who had surmounted many barriers to aviation in the grim period before the war, remained on the periphery of the American aviation community. Robinson's story is a pivotal one, largely because he demonstrated that one path for talented black aviators in the Golden Age of flight—admittedly the most difficult for blacks—was to go abroad to fly. John Robinson chose Africa, his ancestral continent, and this makes his life experience unusual and compelling for us.

National Air & Space Museum                    Von Hardesty
Smithsonian Institution                    Dominick Pisano
Washington, D.C.

# Africa, 1954

The flight had begun with a call to deliver medical supplies to an outlying town. A young Ethiopian had been injured in an aircraft accident and needed blood. The colonel decided to take this flight himself. His friend and former flying student, Biachi Bruno, an Italian engineer, had asked to go along as copilot. He sat in the right seat of the single-engine plane. The flight out had been normal, at least normal for flights over the high and rugged terrain of the African plateau region of Ethiopia. Even now in the fifties this was the kind of bush flying most pilots in the States would consider anything but normal. The colonel didn't need the sophisticated radio navigation aids of modern aviation. He knew the terrain of Ethiopia better than any pilot alive. In fact, there was a time when he remained alive only because he had memorized the valleys, streams, mountains, lowlands, deserts and even rocks and trails of this rough terrain.

Bruno was flying the return trip. The colonel looked over at him and smiled. How many times had Italian pilots tried to kill him, and here he was flying with one he himself had taught to fly. Well, it was like his daddy used to say, "This ole world keeps changin' all the time, too slow for some, too fas' for others." Changed too slowly over here, he thought, but this Italian is here to build, not destroy. And that's a hell of a change from the way it once was. The colonel looked down at the land beneath them. How good this rugged, sometimes savage, beautiful and varied country had been to him, this adopted land ten thousand miles from home.

His attention quickly returned to the flight. What had broken his thoughts? He wasn't sure, but his pilot senses were now registering mild alarm. Something about the engine, the vibrations in the cockpit, was vaguely different. He scanned the engine instruments.

Bruno apparently had not noticed. He was concentrating on doing a smooth job of piloting to impress his old flying instructor.

The engine noise changed faintly but noticeably. The tachometer needle began to wiggle. This time Bruno sensed something had changed. He opened his mouth to speak but the engine spoke first with the kind of metal to metal pounding that sends pilots into red alert.

Both men reached for the fuel selector. The colonel was first and switched tanks, checked both mag switches and pulled the throttle back to reduce stress on what was left of the engine. It was knocking like a trip hammer on a boilerplate. The instrument panel and control wheel were vibrating violently.

Unbeknownst to the two men a valve stem had fractured moments before. The intake valve had stuck open for a few seconds, then dropped into the cylinder where the piston slammed into it, driving it through the top of the cylinder. The piston pounded itself to pieces, bending the rod. The engine maintained partial power, enough to keep the plane flying, but it continued to pump fuel and oil past the broken piston and out of the cracked cylinder head onto the hot engine.

Bruno asked, "What now, my friend?" He tried to smile through his fear.

The colonel looked at the ground below. He turned the plane slightly and searched behind them. "We can try to put it down, but I don't think we stand a chance in hell of doing it in one piece. I figure we're about eight or ten minutes out. With a little luck, this engine will hold together for ten more minutes and we'll make it."

"And if we're not so lucky?" asked Bruno.

"The engine will quit or catch fire, or both, and we'll have to put it down anyway, in which case my little Momma might turn out to be right after all these years."

"Your mother?"

"Just something she said to me a long time ago."

# Mississippi, 1910

A crowd had gathered at the foot of Twenty-third Avenue on East Beach to view, for the first time in Gulfport—perhaps in the whole state of Mississippi—a flying machine and its already famous pilot, John Moisant.

Moisant had recently returned from Europe where he had won an air race in Paris. He had flown to the coast of Mississippi from New Orleans to see the booming new town of Gulfport.

Both the railroad and the harbor were built by Joseph T. Jones, a Pennsylvania oil man.

Jones' daughter stood on the beach laughing and talking with Moisant while her friend Elsie Gary sat on the wing of the frail Pusher bi-plane, made even more awkward looking by the large float attached to its underside. Miss Jones turned to Moisant, "Take us flying, John." She smiled and added, "Please."

Elsie cried, "Oh! Yes, but my daddy will just die."

"Mine will kill me, but Elsie, let's do it! Please John, will you take us?"

The toss of a coin decided that Elsie would go first. She borrowed a jacket from someone in the crowd and put on John's spare leather helmet and goggles. Thus, properly attired, eighteen-year-old Elsie Gary became the first known air passenger in the state of Mississippi.

Among the excited spectators who witnessed this grand event was a seven-year-old boy, who stood at the edge of the crowd. When the engine of the plane burst loudly to life, the boy clutched the hand of his mother, a small heavyset black woman. Standing near the water's edge at the back of the crowd, they could see little.

Moisant signaled for the men who had waded into the water to let go of the plane. It struggled across the water into the southeast breeze, blowing swirls of spray until at last it lifted into the air. Over the harbor it turned and came low down the beach past the crowd. The boy's small brown face, eyes wide, mouth open, stared up in awe. Then he broke from his mother and ran down the beach with hands stretched high as if reaching to touch the plane, jumping and running after the strange flying machine with joy and wonder in his eyes and laughter on his lips. This black child's name was John Charles Robinson and he had found his impossible dream.

Born in Carabelle, Florida, in 1903, he moved with his mother to Gulfport after the death of his father. His mother, Celest, remarried. Her new husband was Charles Cobb, a mechanic employed by the Gulf and Ship Island Railroad at its big shop in Gulfport.

Johnny could not wait for Charles Cobb to get home that day. He thought of him as his daddy. He sat on the corner in front of his house looking down the road which led toward the G & SI Railroad shops. The house was a two-story wood frame building with half brick and half wood columns across the front porch. It was large, and Celest Cobb rented several rooms to boarders. It stood —and still stands—in what was referred to as "the Big Quarter" on the west side of town. Many blacks owned their own homes in Gulfport at a time when this was uncommon in the South. This was due to the relatively good wages paid by the railroad, as well as the decent pay earned by the stevedores at the port. It was a new town, booming with the timber trade. By 1910 Gulfport boasted a population of 10,000. The town had an electric company, streetcars, waterworks, a sewer system, paved streets and eighteen passenger trains serviced it each day.

John could always pick out his father from the other men walking far down the street. Charles Cobb walked with a limp, the result of a shop accident that had crushed his leg. John saw him and ran two blocks to tell, in wide-eyed excitement, about the flying machine he had seen that day.

When the two arrived home, Mr. Cobb picked up Johnny's sister, Bertha, and together they joined Celest in the kitchen for supper. He listened to Johnny talk about the aeroplane and wondered if someday he would have to try to explain to this child he loved that a black man had about as much chance of flying as he himself had of being an engineer for the railroad. He tried to remember when he had finally accepted the fact that he would never drive a steam engine. Well, he had never been able to give up the dream entirely. That's why he had become a railroad mechanic, working his way up from laborer and gandy dancer. If he couldn't drive one, he would work on them and keep them running. Lord, they still thrilled him, and he must have been about Johnny's age when he saw his first steam locomotive.

As the years passed there was very little doubt about John Robinson's continued interest in all things mechanical, but especially in aeroplanes. The great war burst across Europe, and headlines about planes and daring pilots covered the pages of newspapers and magazines.

Johnny read them all. When there was time between school and chores at home, he would whittle out model planes or sometimes build kites, which he flew on the beach front.

One clear fall afternoon Celest stepped off the streetcar which ran along the beach and saw Johnny sitting near the water's edge. Tied to his ankle was a long string leading up to a large white kite floating high on the dying afternoon breeze. The sun, a great orange ball, was just touching the western horizon.

Celest was about to call to him when the kite caught her eye. The brilliant sunset was suddenly reflected on the fluttering white kite and it seemed for an instant to burst into flames and then to sink to earth as the breeze died away. Suddenly she felt a cold shiver of fear and called out to her son, almost running to him. He looked up at her, surprised. He was even more puzzled as she spoke sharply, almost angrily, "You get yourself home, John Robinson. You've got more to do than sit down here playing with a kite and dreaming 'bout aeroplanes and such foolishness. You got to get yo' mind on yo' schoolwork and makin' somethin' of yo'self. Daddy Cobb is working hard and extra and so am I to help you get to college. You are fourteen and you are old enough to get yo' attention on important things."

"Why are you so mad at me, Momma," John asked "What's wrong?" Celest did not know. Her anger had covered the unexplained feeling of fear she had felt watching the kite. She put her arm around him and said, "I'm just tired, I guess, and I'm gonna be late getting Daddy's supper if we don't get home. Here, you carry the groceries and I'll carry the kite." "I guess I don't like to see my boy gittin' so big. Won't be long before you'll be leaving us to go out in the world on yo' own. I just want you to learn a good trade so you'll be ready, so you can make a real place for yourself."

"It's okay, Momma, I'm gonna work hard at school."

"Well, yo' daddy and me are gonna do everything we can to help get you to Tuskegee Institute, but you gonna have to help yo'self and put away all that dreamin' 'bout flyin'. It scares me, son, and besides, the truth is no black man is gonna get a chance to do no flyin'. You old enough to know that."

In silence they walked on towards their home past the neatly painted frame houses of the white middle class and on into the Big Quarter with its mixture of small

frame structures, some painted, some with bare weathered siding. Few had grass yards in front, though many
had small gardens and chicken yards out back. Here and
there along the street there was an occasional small
enterprise such as a grocery or a clothing shop. In a frame
house across the street from the Cobb home was the
J. T. Hall Undertaking Company, which had just opened.

As they reached the corner, a small boy about ten was
playing with a tireless bicycle wheel, rolling it down the
hard dirt street with a stick. "Hey, Marcus," called
Johnny. "Come here a minute, I got something for you."
Marcus controlled the wheel with his stick so that it
made a perfect turn over to where Johnny and his mother
were standing.

"Hey, Johnny, what you got fo' me?"

"You like this kite I made don't you?"

"Oh! Yea! Man, but you ain't giving it to me is ya?"

Johnny took the kite from his mother and handed it
to Marcus. "Here, you take it, an' don't you let it get
hung up on no trees." Marcus carefully took the kite and
ball of string with one hand and his old bicycle wheel in
the other.

"Man, thank you, Johnny, it's the neatest kite there
is." Marcus turned and started across the street. He
yelled at a friend a half block away, "Hey, Alfred, look
here what Johnny give me, look at this, man!"

"You didn't have to do that, son," Celest Cobb said.

"Yea I did, Mom, 'cause you're right. I'm almost
fifteen. I want to get a job, help you and Daddy get me
to school. "After thinking a moment he added, "But
you're wrong 'bout one thing, Momma, someday this
black man gonna fly!"

# Tough Shine

It was already dark when they reached home. Charles Cobb was sitting on the porch rolling a cigarette. "Where ya'll been? I was starting to worry, not to mention getting hungry," he laughed. "I already picked up Bertha and we even got the stove hot."

"I'm sorry, Honey," Celest said, "I was late with the shopping. I'll warm up some gumbo, and some hot bread to go with it."

Charles carefully pulled the drawstring tight on his tobacco bag, then put it and his package of cigarette paper into the top pocket of his bib overalls. Holding a match which he lit with his thumb nail, he fired his handrolled cigarette and took a deep drag. "Nothing better than y'all's gumbo, Darling. What you got to say for yo'self, Johnny?"

"Nothing, Daddy, 'cept I'm gonna look for a job to help with my school money. I figure I can shine shoes at Union Station or maybe on the corner by the Parlor Drug Store."

Charles looked at Johnny. "You and Momma must been talking mighty serious talk."

"Naw, Daddy, I just figure being almost fifteen, it's time I did something on my own. And I'd like to come down to the shop with you and learn more 'bout machinery and things. Maybe I could get a job sweeping down there or something."

Charles Cobb put his arm around the stepson he loved as his own. "That would be fine, son. Now, let's go in and light a fire. I think it's going to be right chilly tonight. Maybe after supper you can read me the paper 'bout the war and how our boys are doing over there, and 'bout those airplane fights. This world is in a real mess, but some mighty interesting things are happening. You keep up with things, Johnny; the world's changin' for colored folks too. Yes, sir, you keep up with it, boy. Now let's go see 'bout supper."

All the next week Johnny looked for a spot to shine shoes. He found however that all the best corners and the train station too were already spoken for by a healthy number of shoeshine boys, most of whom were older and larger than himself. After losing three fights over shoeshine territories, he decided to look elsewhere for a job.

The following Monday he dressed in his Sunday clothes, took the sack lunch his mother had fixed for him, and walked the short distance to the three-room school on Thirty-second Avenue. It was a wood frame building in need of paint. Inside it was clean, the bare wood floors smelled of linseed oil and in the center room there stood a large potbellied stove. There were black-boards in each of the other two rooms. A small one-room building next door, called "The Annex," was used for elementary school.

As Johnny went into the schoolyard, a small girl ran over to him. "You sho' dressed up, Johnny Robinson, just like when you walk me to Sunday School. What you dressed up for." They were joined by a boy Johnny's age. "Yea, John," said the boy wearing overalls, no shirt, and no shoes. "You gonna make points with the teacher, or you been struck by love or something. You sho' ain't gonna play no baseball after school in that git-up."

"Now don't you go messin' with me, Alexander. I'm dressed up 'cause I'm going downtown to look for a job after school, and as for you, Miomi Godine, you get yo'self over to the annex where you belong. The only reason I take you to Sunday School is 'cause my momma and yo' momma are friends and they ask me to look after you."

"Aw man, we don't mean nothing. How come you always gotta be so serious?", asked Alexander.

"I just got things I gotta do, and getting my first job is one of 'em."

Two weeks passed before Johnny Robinson got his first job. It was sweeping floors, cleaning the stockroom and delivering packages by bicycle for the Bee Hive Department Store on Fourteenth Street in downtown Gulfport. He worked after school and on Saturdays.

The year was 1918 and halfway around the world another young black man was busy at his first job. The man was twenty-six-year-old Ras Tafari Makonnen, second cousin to the daughter of the late Menelik II, Zaudith, now Empress of Ethiopia.

He had been appointed by the ailing empress to be the ruling regent of Ethiopia. This land was once known as Abyssinia, and before 1,000 B.C. was called Aksum. Fate would one day place these two black men together, one to serve the other, each to be the other's friend.

# Northbound

**B**y the summer of 1920 John was showing the characteristics that were to carry him so far. He was tall for his age. Though his expression was usually serious, when he did smile or laugh, there was honest joy in it. He carried himself confidently but there was also a warmth about him that made him immediately likeable.

Most Sundays he attended the African Methodist Episcopal Church, a small building at the corner of Thirty-second Avenue and Twenty-first Street. The minister of the church, his school principal, Pastor Lanoa, encouraged him to go to Tuskegee Institute in Alabama.

On a Sunday afternoon in late August, Johnny walked aimlessly down Thirty-first Avenue to the beach and turned east toward town. He thought about going to Tuskegee and about leaving home for the first time. He passed the electric power plant at the foot of Thirtieth Avenue; black smoke poured from the tall brick chimney. Out at the port he could see steam and sailing ships. For the first time steamships were beginning to outnumber the tall masted barks and brigantines.

He watched the streetcars running back and forth out to the pavillion at the end of the earth-filled pier. Sunday strollers moved along the boardwalk, which paralleled the tracks. A boxcar was being loaded with ice at the big ice house as Johnny turned north toward downtown Gulfport. He picked up a broken chip of ice and chewed it as he walked.

On Sunday afternoons he had always liked to go downtown to watch the increasing number of automobiles. They were beginning to replace the horse-drawn

12

buggies, just as steamships were replacing those powered by sail. There was a Miller Tire and Gasoline store not far from the Alexander Livery, Harness, and Vehicle Company. There were even two motorcycles in town.

Johnny turned off Twenty-fifth Avenue at the Parlor Drugstore and walked west on Fourteenth Street past the Hewes Brothers Building. He turned on Twenty-seventh Avenue at the Inn Hotel and crossed over to Union Station, which was always a center of activity: locomotives moving through, people coming and going, wagons and trucks loading or unloading. Soon it was going to be his turn to get on a train and leave this town he called home. Gulfport was a good town, he thought. For the most part, he liked the people, both black and white. Now he had finished high school, which only went to the tenth grade, and he was leaving. His daddy was right, John thought. Things were changing in the world, and he was going to do his best to keep up with them. He was tall, he was black, a little afraid at the thought of leaving his Mississippi home, and he was seventeen.

The day he left for Tuskegee, Celest Cobb washed, pressed, and packed Johnny's clothes in a small worn trunk. She tucked a small Bible in last as well as a little extra house money she had been saving.

Then she went down to the kitchen and put sandwiches, cookies, and a polished red apple into a brown paper bag.

"Charles," she called, "We better go. He can't miss his train."

Celest and Charles Cobb, and many of Johnny's friends accompanied him to the train station. They waved to him as the train pulled out of the station.

"You can cry now, Momma, if you want to," Charles said as he wiped the corners of his eyes.

Arm in arm they walked home. "Our boy is leaving

home, but I'm so proud we're sending him to college. You're a good man, Charles Cobb."

John Robinson watched the countryside slide by as he gazed out the open train window. He was in the coach at the front of the train just behind the baggage and mail cars. A little more soot and smoke from the engine filtered through the open windows into the front car normally set aside for blacks, but John didn't think much about the dirt and grime collecting on the window sill. He liked being up front where he could hear the rumbling power of the locomotive. It was fire and steam and steel, motion and excitement, and it took his mind off leaving home and thoughts of what lay ahead.

John had read about Tuskegee. He knew the school had been founded by a man, born a slave in Virginia, who at age sixteen walked almost five hundred miles to get an education at the Hampton Institute in 1872. The man was Booker Taliaferro Washington. In 1881 he opened a school with thirty pupils in a church. Now Johnny was on his way to that school, Tuskegee Institute. Booker T. Washington had died in 1915, but an equally famous man was there on campus: George Washington Carver whose research in agricultural chemistry had won him international fame and whose artistic ability had resulted in his election as a Fellow in the Royal Society of Arts in London.

John looked out the train window at an automobile racing along a road beside the railroad tracks. It had no top, and the windscreen was folded down flat. The goggled driver was giving it all he had down a smooth stretch of dirt road. His car kicked up dust and ran down a flock of chickens as he raced the train but it easily outdistanced him. Johnny's daddy had told him that now the war was over the automobile was the coming thing. Johnny believed him. And though he didn't say it, he

believed something more. The war was over and aeroplanes were coming too.

At Tuskegee Normal and Industrial Institute, John
Robinson majored in automotive mechanics. He had
traveled to his college by steam engine and wagon. By
the time he left, he and some friends had put together
an automobile. Very few young men knew more about
auto engines than this quiet, tall, brown-skinned young
man.

Engines, mechanics, and automobiles were all the rage
in 1920. John had a natural mechanical ability that
distinguished him from the other students but he was
so quiet and serious that years later some of his
classmates had a hard time remembering John Robinson
until they saw his picture in the newspapers.

However, the young ladies of Tuskegee didn't over-
look the tall, quiet student from Gulfport. Besides
mechanical skill he developed the ability to excel on the
dance floor. He also developed a sort of shy yet confident
manner that served him well all his life and which,
incidentally, charmed ladies of all ages.

Although an average student in English and math, he
was near the top of his class in mechanical science.
During the week he studied and worked with engines.
On weekends, for fun, he played with them.

Summers he worked at whatever jobs he could find at
home on the coast, saving his pay to help his parents
with his school expenses.

And then there was that wonderful day in 1924 when
Celest and Charles Cobb saw their boy graduate from
Tuskegee.

John was glad to get home that summer. His mother's
gumbo was as good as ever. There was also the little girl
he used to walk to Sunday School. He called her Kitty.
It was nice to be home, but the longer he stayed the
more restless he became.

"We're proud of you, son. You've done so fine at school. And now you are an automotive mechanic right when the streets are starting to fill up with automobiles. 'specially those Model T Fords. There's gonna be plenty of work for you, son."

"That's right, Daddy, but not here in Mississippi."

His father glanced up quickly. "Why, son, there's not more than three garages right here that know what they are doing."

"That's right, Daddy, and I've talked to every one of them. They would give me a job sweeping, or filling gas, or washing, but I'm an engine man, Daddy, and all the cars belong to whites, and I just don't think I'm gonna get the chance to do here at home what I know I can do." John's voice was even and quiet.

"Son, me and you are colored, but there are some fine white folks here that will give you a chance if you'll just give 'em a little time to learn what you can do. I don't exactly sweep floors over at the railroad shops. You know that. And yo' Momma and I haven't done too bad. We own this house, we educated you and your sister."

"I know, Daddy, and I'm grateful to you, and more proud of you and Momma than you can ever know, but I want my own business, and I can't do it down here. There just wouldn't be enough business for a colored man's mechanic shop. "I guess what I'm trying to say is that I got to go to the North for a chance to really put my training to use. I'm going to Detroit, Daddy. There's a friend from school I can stay with 'til I get started. You gonna help me tell Momma?"

Charles Cobb put an arm around the tall slim man standing next to him. "I've been helping you tell yo' Momma things for a long time, Son. I guess we'll go in and tell her together."

# Taste the Wind

Upon his arrival in Detroit, Johnny discovered that getting started in his own business would take a little longer than he had first thought. There was certainly a great deal of automotive activity in that industrial city. That was part of the problem. There was so much emphasis on automotive development in Detroit that a young black man from the Gulf Coast of Mississippi found it hard to convince anyone he had come from the South already well trained and experienced in the field of automotive mechanics.

He was determined to get a job as a mechanic, not as a sweeper, or errand boy. It took him six weeks to do it, but he finally got a position as assistant mechanic at a large shop housed in what had been a livery stable and saddle store. Including himself, there were seven mechanics. The shop also had a manager who doubled as a tire and parts salesman, and a younger man who pumped gas.

John found that, of the six mechanics, all white, two were friendly, three didn't seem to notice him at all, and one was openly hostile towards him. He also discovered that the "assistant mechanic" got to do a lot of tire changing and was mostly called upon to work on the automobiles of black customers that occasionally appeared at the shop. He spent most of his time acting as a pair of "extra hands" for the other mechanics.

After some months had passed, the mechanics in the shop began to notice and admit two things about John Robinson. The first was that he could learn from them and learn quickly. The second was that they in turn were learning some things from him. There was rarely a complaint about his work, and customers were beginning to ask specifically for him to do the work on their cars. Eight months after he started work the word "assistant" was dropped from the job title on his pay envelope, and he found more money inside it.

A lot of things were beginning to fall into line for J. C. Robinson. He now owned a car, or rather a collection of automobile parts he had skillfully turned into a motor car. He had moved from a boarding house to a three-room flat with a kitchen, a small sitting room and a smaller bedroom. His flat was equipped with electric lights and an oil stove for heat and cooking.

Although he was already earning the name "tight-lipped Robinson" because he rarely talked unless he had something to say, he could let it all go on a dance floor, which he often did on Saturday nights.

The ladies were not slow to notice this tall, quiet, dancing man, whose smooth, confident manner and neat dress attracted them, even in the flashy age of flappers and jazz.

The girls knew Johnny was in town, but he was not about to settle in Detroit, as more than a few who tried to change his mind, found out. There was a restlessness about him that, to the few who knew him well, seemed more than just a desire to be good at his trade. Books on mechanics, and those dealing with "running your own business," were growing in number at that time. He lined a long shelf in his sitting room with them. John knew the cause of his restlessness. He had been able to put it away for all those years of school. Besides, he had promised his mother that he would put away what she referred to as "that foolishness." For the most part he had kept that promise.

But during those years there was little he could do to keep his heart from jumping whenever he heard the sound of an engine overhead. He would look upwards with the anticipation of a child at Christmas, in hopes of catching a glimpse of the aircraft high overhead. He still did, only now there were more aeroplanes up there and more in the news too—new aviation records were being made every week. A few books on aviation engines and aeroplane design appeared on his bookshelf. John knew what was pushing inside him. He just didn't know what to do about it.

After all, only the army-trained barnstorming air gypsies from the Great War or a handful of government and business personnel or wealthy white playboys or such other "mad fools" actually worked or played with aircraft. How in the hell would a black man do it when, to his knowledge, no black men were even working on aeroplanes, much less flying them?

There were plenty of people, black as well as white, who would tell you a black man was physically incapable of acquiring aeronautic skills, or adjusting to the environment of flight. With these thoughts in mind, John Robinson finally admitted to himself that he could not go all his life without knowing whether he would ever find the joy and excitement he had always felt must be a part of flight.

He decided it was time. Once he finally made that decision, he felt a calm satisfaction, "Yes, sir," he said out loud, "it's time I found out."

One Sunday morning he drove to the outskirts of Detroit to a small field where a faded red, white, and blue banner strung on a fence invited one to "Take an Aeroplane Ride with an Ace."

Johnny had deliberately picked the small field near Willow Run and Ypsilanti instead of Detroit City Airport or Ford Field. He thought he might get a longer ride for his money if he flew in a rural area where business was slower. He also admitted to himself that there might be less chance of his being turned down. One thing he had found out was that his daddy had been right when he had said that the South was not the only place where a black man's money sometimes wouldn't buy the same things as a white man's money.

He parked beside the fence and followed the well-worn path around to the front of the hangars. He could see three aeroplanes inside, or rather two and a half, since the one in the middle was missing one wing and its engine. John recognized that one, and the one nearest him, which had all its parts, but didn't look much better. They were both Curtiss JN-4D's, better known as Jennys.

It was the third plane that caught his eye. It was bright red, and clean as a whistle. To Johnny it was beautiful. He walked over to it and touched its wing the way a child would touch the glass window of a candy shop. He still had seen no one else on the field. He walked around the wing and stood by the rear cockpit and looked inside. His eyes took in the whole plane as well as each part separately: the instruments, the rudder bar and the stick, the seat belt, all so different from the automobiles and the motorcycles he had driven. He walked back around to the front of the plane and studied the engine. Like the Jennys, he saw that it had an OX5 water-cooled engine. Well, thought John, at least this was something he understood. Engines were engines, and this one was not much different from those he had worked on in cars or trucks at the shop.

"Hey, you, boy! What the hell are you doing around that plane?"

John swung around to face a short, heavily built, redheaded man with grease stains on his face. He was dressed in soiled khaki pants and a leather jacket. In one hand he held a wrench and in the other a rag. Behind him was a younger man, cleanly dressed in riding boots, riding britches, a blue sweater and tie. The young man had a smile on his face. The redheaded man didn't.

Startled, John stood speechless for a moment.

"Well, boy?" the redhead said. He had a slight Irish accent.

"I came out here to get an aeroplane ride; is this the right place? Nobody was around so I was just looking," John said. "I didn't touch anything", he added.

"Yea, this is the right place, if that's why you're really here. Why did you come all the way out here, anyway? Wouldn't they give a nigger a ride at the big city airport?"

John, although outwardly quiet, was never one to hold his temper too long, and he was struggling with himself to hold it now. "Look, mister, I just came out here to pay for an aeroplane ride. I got the money same as anyone else, I want to see what it's like, that's all."

"Aw, come on, Percy, what the hell you being so grumpy for?" said the younger man looking at Johnny. "He's had a bad week, his engine is down, and he's a redheaded Irishman." He added, "Come on, Percy, drop the whole thing, I'll drive you into town for a beer."

"Why not, I can't make a dime standing here," replied Percy. The two men turned to walk away. "Hey, wait a minute," called Johnny. "Maybe I can fix the trouble. If I can, I'll do it for a flight."

"Now what do you know about aeroplanes, boy?"

"My name's John Robinson, and I don't know any-thing about aeroplanes, but I know something about en-gines, I'm a mechanic."

"Sure," replied Percy. He kept walking without look-ing back.

"Percy," said the younger man with a laugh, "You're acting like what my father says all Irishmen are, butt-headed, stubborn, rude, and with bigger fists than brains."

"In that case, I'll buy my own beer, and you can take your new little red playtoy and shove it in someone else's hangar."

John hadn't moved. He could still hear them talking though they had disappeared around the side of the hangar walking toward the fence.

"Come on, Percy. You can't afford to buy beer. You're down to one worn-out Jenny with a broken engine. You're too Irish proud to let me help you out. You can't get a job with any of the new outfits 'cause you got drunk and took your boss's daughter flying, under a bridge, for Christ's sake. And now you won't even find out if maybe this guy is telling the truth and can put you back in business in time to make a few bucks this afternoon."

Percy stopped, looked at his companion, and without a word, turned and walked around the hangar and up to Johnny. "What kind of mechanic are you?"

"Automotive."

"How did you get to be a mechanic?"

"Three years of college, and I been working nearly two years in Detroit. I built that car out there myself."

"Do you know how to do brazing work and do you have an outfit?"

"I can get an outfit at the shop in town," Johnny replied.

Percy moved over to the engine of his Jenny. "Come here and look at this. You see the crack, just a hairline crack in the water jacket right there. As soon as this thing gets good and hot, water starts spewing out of that crack and fouls the ignition system. It quit six times before I found the trouble. By the time I got it on the ground the water jacket would cool, the leak would stop, and the ignition would dry out. The thing would start the first try and then it would fly fine for about fifteen minutes and quit again. All OX5 engines should all be sold to the Navy for anchors. Anyway, boy, you get that brazing outfit out here and fix this crack and I'll give you the ride you want. But you screw up this engine and I'll put more than a hairline crack in your water jacket, so you better know what you're doing or don't screw with it."

John didn't like the term, "boy", and he didn't care much for the ill-tempered Percy, but he figured he had a chance to do two things. One was to fly for the first time. The other was to show the redheaded bigot that a black mechanic could put him back in business.

"It's a deal."

It was three-thirty in the afternoon when they rolled the faded yellow Jenny out of the hangar. "Well, John Robinson, your work is pretty enough. Now let's see if it holds. You stand back while Robert here gives me a crank. Will you do that, Robert?"

Robert Williamson, John had learned, was fresh out of college and had returned to Detroit to work for his father, who owned a manufacturing firm. Percy had taught him how to fly, a fact Robert's father still did not know, and Robert had just bought the red plane with money his grandfather had left him.

"O.K. Switch off, throttle closed," called Robert.

"Off and closed," Percy replied.

Robert turned the wooden propeller over several times and called, "Switch on. Contact."

"Contact," repeated Percy.

Robert put both hands up on the prop. swung his right leg up towards the plane. As he swung his leg down he heaved with both hands to turn the prop through. At the same moment, the momentum of his right leg swinging behind him carried him away from the propeller, swinging him around to the point where he could run several steps away and to the side. Although the tail skid would generally hold a plan in place while the engine idled, the Jenny had no brakes. Should the throttle be inadvertently left open while cranking, the plane could easily run down anyone careless enough to stand around in front of it after propping the engine.

After three more attempts, the engine coughed, burped, spit twice, and roared alive, settling down to a more or less smooth rumble.

Robert grabbed hold of the outer wing strut on one side and motioned for Johnny to do the same on the other wing. Percy, after checking to see that his two anchor men were all set, slowly opened the throttle. The grass behind the Jenny flattened. Dust and loose grass swirled up as the plane shook from wing tip to tail and began to pull both Robert and John forward. Percy closed the throttle and pulled the fuel mixture control to the off position. The field was suddenly quiet again, except for the excited chatter of a carload of people who had driven up to the fence while the engine was roaring away. Percy climbed out of the cockpit and carefully examined the waterjacket and the ignition wiring of the engine.

"I've got to admit, it looks like you've done a good job."

Johnny hardly had a chance to break into a grin before a voice from the fence called, "Hey, Percy, quit fooling around over there, I've brought the whole Sunday School out to take rides with you."

The voice belonged to a young lady waving from a second car that had just driven up.

"Come on, Percy, dear, all eleven of us want a ride." She stepped down from the car and came through the gate followed by four other girls and six young men.

"Sue said you shot down a German in 1918. Is that true, Mr. Percy?" one of the other girls asked.

Percy tried not to look embarrassed, and the more he tried the closer his face came to matching his flaming red hair. He took a handkerchief from his back pocket and tried to wipe the oil from his face and hands.

"Well, young lady, it's too pretty an afternoon to talk about that sort of thing. Sue, why don't you draw straws to see what order you'll fly in while we get some fuel." He motioned to Robert and Johnny to follow him over to where several barrels of gasoline were lying on a wooden rack. He picked up a five gallon can with a spout on it and began to fill it from one of the barrels.

"Come on," said Johnny, "I mean, what about our deal, I've done my part."

"So you have," replied Percy, "and I'll take you for a ride but I can't do it right now. You can see the situation here. I mean I can't take you for a ride and make them sit over there and wait. Can't you understand what I'm trying to say?"

"Sure, I understand what you're trying to say. You're trying to say you can't make that nice Sunday School class wait around for a turn while you take a nigger for a ride. Isn't that what you're trying to say?"

Percy turned blood-red in the face and Robert stepped between the two.

"Percy shouted, "Damn you, boy, can't you understand anything. If I hadn't given you my word on this deal I'd split your head wide open for a crack like that. There are eleven people over there. At five dollars apiece that's fifty-five dollars. I can buy a new Army surplus engine for fifty dollars. Hell, there are more people waiting over there than came out here all last week."

Johnny looked past Robert straight at Percy, but remained silent.

"Look," said Percy, "I got six dollars in my pocket. You take five dollars for fixing my engine, or you come back when I ain't got a line of people waiting."

"I don't want your money, I want to fly. I want to fly more than all eleven of those people over there."

"And I need that fifty-five dollars to stay in business."

"O.K., both of you," said Robert J. Williamson III. "The solution is simple. You go fly the Sunday School class, and I'll take our friend John here flying in my plane in exchange for two free lessons in stunt flying from you."

"Robinson, will you settle for thirty minutes with me instead of five minutes with him, even though I'm too young to have any Germans to my credit?"

All three men exchanged glances. Robert was the first to smile. Percy looked quizzically at Johnny, who looked over his shoulder at the red plane waiting in the hangar. He turned back to the pair standing in front of him. In spite of all he could do, John broke into a wide grin, and laughed out loud, "You white boys just made yo'selves a deal."

They topped off the Jenny and helped Percy settle his first passenger of the day into the front cockpit. The engine was still warm and it fired on the first swing of the prop. To a round of applause, the Jenny waddled off over the grass, her waddle changing to bumps and bounces as she gained speed, finally smoothing out as she lifted into the air and labored up over the trees at the end of the field.

"All right, John, let's roll the Waco out." Robert motioned for John to move behind the right wing and push on the outer wing strut while Robert did the same on the left side. Compared to the cat's cradle maze of struts and bracing wires that strung the wings of the Jenny together, the Waco Nine had a sleek and uncluttered design. Although she used the same army surplus OX5 engine as the standard Jenny (as did many postwar designs because it was plentiful and cheap —though it was often also heavy and unreliable), the clean lines of the Waco and its strong steel-tube fuselage gave it far better performance than the Jenny and many other production planes of the day. Bright with its new crimson paint, it was the most beautiful thing Johnny had ever seen.

Robert Williamson had used $2,475.50 of the rather sizable sum left him by his grandfather to pay for it. Of the one-hundred-and-six flying hours to his credit, the last twenty-five had been logged in the Waco.

"Well, John, let's walk around her and I'll explain anything you want to know while I check things out. I haven't had a problem yet. I had six forced landings in that damn Jenny, four of them with Percy, and two by myself. The radiator doesn't even leak yet." (The radiator was mounted in front of the cockpits, just under the top wing. If it leaked, as most radiators did, it leaked hot, rusty water that blew back on both passenger and pilot.)

John had so many questions that Robert finally protested, "If we don't get going Percy will have us fueling him up again and acting as his ticket takers. Besides, for a guy that's never flown, you seem to know a lot about planes. Most people wouldn't even know what questions to ask."

"I guess I been reading about 'em as long as I can remember," replied Johnny, "but this is the first time I've been up close. I mean, it's really gonna happen isn't it?"

Robert grinned at him. "Not if you don't get up in that front cockpit. Put on this pair of goggles. I don't have an extra helmet." He made sure John's harness was fastened. "When I say contact, and not before, you turn on that switch. And keep this throttle back or this thing might fire up, then run over me, and take you God knows where. And remember to hold the stick back all the way. Now you got it?"

"I got it." John was excited. He was also more than a little afraid but he managed to look calm. At least he thought so until Robert said, "Relax, John, if you don't loosen your grip on that stick, your black hand is going to turn as white as mine. Remember, flying takes a light touch." With that he jumped off the wing and moved around front where he could crank the propeller.

He turned the prop around several times and then called, "Contact." On the second try the engine fired, missed, fired again, and settled down to a ka-puck-a-ta, puck-a-ta rhythm that gently rocked the plane. The smell of hot oil filled the front cockpit as Robert climbed up on the wing and leaned over Johnny.

"While we are up I'm going to let you try your hand at it. If I wiggle the stick like this," and he moved the stick quickly side to side several times, "it means you can take over and fly. If I wiggle it while you have it, it means for you to let go, that I will take it. I won't be able to hear you, so if everything is all right, or if we do something and you want to do it again, put your thumb up like this. If you don't like it, shake your head from side to side. If you want to come down, point down at the field, You got it?"

John started to answer, then grinned and held his thumb up. Robert slapped him on the back and climbed into the rear cockpit. He fastened his safety harness, buckled on his flying helmet and began to taxi downwind to the end of the field. There he stopped, tested the controls, ran the engine up to make sure it would develop full power. (There was no way to check the ignition system of the OX5. Unlike modern aircraft it did not have dual ignition. If it was running, then the single ignition system was working.)

Percy floated over them in the Jenny. Then he settled to the ground, and taxied toward his eager group of waiting passengers.

Robert called to Johnny, "You ready?" Johnny nodded his head and was about to answer when Robert pushed the throttle forward, feeding in rudder to counteract the torque of the engine in order to hold a straight takeoff roll. Johnny's answer was lost in the wind. The roar and vibration of the heavy OX5 filled the cockpit, the blast from its sweeping wooden propeller washing over him, laden with the oily smells of the hot engine. As the Waco accelerated, Robert eased the stick slightly forward and the tail lifted. Now Johnny could see ahead as the grass rushed beneath the bouncing wheels. The trees at the far end of the field grew nearer. He held tightly to the sides of the cockpit. Robert eased the stick back and the bumping and bouncing of the wheels against the uneven turf ceased as the Waco, its red wings turning to gold in the late afternoon sun of autumn, climbed into the sky.

John watched the field drop away as all below seemed to turn miniature except for the earth itself which expanded in all directions as they climbed.

He remembered that day as a child when he had run with excitement and joy down the beach after the first aeroplane he had ever seen, and now that same childlike joy and wonder and excitement rushed over him, filling him, fulfilling him.

They circled in the crisp clear air which was much cooler at 3,000 feet than it was on the ground. To the northeast they could see the industrial smoke of Detroit hanging over the city. Below lay the small lakes of the Huron and just on the horizon to the southeast they could make out the edge of Lake Erie.

The smoothness of the flight was suddenly interrupted by a slight wavering followed by smoothness followed again by wavering of the wings. Johnny glanced down into the cockpit to see the stick wiggling back and forth from side to side.

He tried to look back at Robert but his safety harness was too tight for him to twist around. The stick wiggled again. John slowly relaxed his grip on the sides of the cockpit and placed his hands on the unfamiliar control stick and wiggled it slightly. Instantly the smooth sure path of flight they had been enjoying changed to a weaving, dipping track through the sky, like a gentle roller coaster ride as Robert released control to the unsteady, unsure, but willing hands of John Robinson. He felt clumsy and embarrassed at his awkward attempt to hold the craft steady. John could keep the wings fairly level but he could not keep the nose from climbing or dropping.

Then the thought struck him. "I'm flying thise thing! It's not too smooth, but man, it's not falling out of the sky, either!" He tried a turn using just the stick to bank the wings. Not much happened, so he tried a turn using just the rudder. Not too much happened that way, either. Then he tried using both the stick and the rudder together and this time he got a pretty good turn though the nose dropped and started the whole gentle roller coaster ride again.

The stick wiggled in his hand and John let it go and returned his hands to the sides of the cockpit. The flight steadied back into a graceful path through the sky as Robert once again took control.

John held his hand in the air with his thumb up. Immediately, the nose of the plane dropped to a steep angle. The wind began to whistle past the bracing wires of the wings as the speed increased in the dive. Johnny's eyes widened and he tightened his grip on the sides of the cockpit. He was suddenly pressed deep into his seat as Robert pulled back on the stick, bringing the nose sharply up. As the horizon came into view Robert gave the engine full throttle and continued to hold the stick back. The plane climbed straight up and then over on its back as it tracked a graceful loop.

"Jesus," whispered Johnny, and then as the plane dove down the back side of the loop he shouted more in exhilaration than fear, "God A'mighty!" Once again he was pressed deep into his seat as Robert pulled out of the dive and back to level flight.

"Yea, oh yea!" hollered John, and he held up both hands with his thumbs straight up. Robert laughed. He entered another loop following it with a sweeping barrel roll, then turned back toward the field. The sun was low on the horizon as they flew downwind. They could see the Jenny taxiing toward the hangar. The last of Percy's passengers were moving along the fence toward their car.

Robert gently banked the Waco, turning upwind in line with the field. The plane, in a glide with its engine throttle-back, passed over the fence. It floated briefly as Robert gently pulled back on the stick, and settled with one soft bounce to the grassy field. After a short landing roll the plane taxied to the hangar, swinging around in one last blast of the engine so that the tail faced the entrance.

Then there was silence, sudden and complete, as the flicking propeller came to rest.

John sat still as though he were afraid he would somehow lose that sweet moment if he moved, like waking from a dream. He was aware of his senses still relating to the flight. His ears rang from the engine's roar; his body relaxed in the absence of the vibrations of powered flight; his goggles now felt uncomfortably tight, and his bare head tingled, his scalp was sore from the wind buffet of the flight; and there was that hot engine smell flooding back over the windshield and into the cockpit.

"Robinson, are you all right?"

"Man," replied Johnny, "I don't think I'm ever gonna get this smile off my face. I mean there's nothing like it, is there? Nothing as free."

"Well, there was this girl I knew once," grinned

Robert. "Now get down out of there and help me get this thing in the hangar."

Together they pushed the Waco, tail first, into the hangar. Then they walked around the hangar toward the fence in time to see Percy driving off with the young Sunday School teacher. Robert walked toward the motorbike leaned against the fence beside Johnny's car.

"Robert, do you think I could learn to fly? I mean, well, I think I can learn, but can I get someone to teach me?"

"Hell, why not," replied Robert. He looked back at John. "Oh, I see, you mean because you're colored. You learned to be a mechanic, didn't you?"

"Yea, but that was at a Negro college. Do you know any Negros that are flying? Any that are teaching?"

"No, but that doesn't mean there aren't any. If you want to learn bad enough, you'll find a way. I did, even though my father tried every way he could to stop me. He owns a factory that makes coffins and he thinks I should, in his words 'make the damn things, not fly in one.' The flying schools here in the city owe money to a bank that happens to have Dad on its board of directors. They got the message and wouldn't teach me. So, I finally found Percy out here. He didn't owe any bank, because no bank would lend him money for that old wreck of his. I had a little money saved so he taught me to fly. The trouble is, he is leaving. The Jenny is outdated. All the schools are getting newer planes. He can't compete and he's broke. He's taken a job flying the mail overnight from New York to Chicago. I think he's crazy. They've killed about twenty pilots with that mail flying already, but he says he has to do that or give up flying. I don't know what to tell you except to go out and try."

"Well, what about you, I'd pay you. Would you teach me?"

"Me? No. I'm afraid I can't do it, John."

"Sure, I understand," Johnny replied, and started to open his car door. "Now hold on. If you're thinking I'm handing you the nigger boy bit you're out of line. I just took you flying, remember. And I'll tell you something else. If every time you don't get the chance to do something, you think it's just because you're colored, you're gonna wind up using that as a crutch not to try. I can't teach you because I'm not qualified in the first place, and in the second place my Waco and I are leaving for Texas. I've got a job with a college buddy drilling for oil, and that sounds better to me than making coffins."

"O.K. I'm sorry. I've been dreaming about flying since I was a kid. I went through plenty of those 'Willie, get away from dat wheelbarrow, you don't know nothing 'bout MACHINERY' jokes when I first started work as a mechanic, and I don't like the idea of starting that all over again with aeroplanes. I guess I'll just start knocking on hangar doors."

"Look," said Robert, "You got a job here, do you think you could get one in Chicago?"

"I guess so. There are plenty of cars need fixin' in Chicago. But why? I'm just gettin' in good shape here."

"Well, if you are going to get rejected by a lot of flying schools, you might as well start with one of the best. That's the Curtiss-Wright Flying School in Chicago. I think they teach aircraft mechanics there, too. Maybe you could work days and go to their school for classroom study at night. If you could get through a school like that, you would be more likely to get some kind of aircraft or flying job. It's an idea you can think about anyway." Robert cranked the motorbike and turned it around. "I wish you luck, John Robinson, I really do."

"Thank you, man, I mean you don't know what flying with you today has meant to me."

Robert grinned. "Yes, I do. There's not a pilot alive who doesn't remember his first flight."

He turned on his headlight, nodded a smile, and disappeared down the dirt road into the falling darkness. John sat alone on the running board of his car. In the stillness of the early evening he thought about his good job. There would be no way to justify, much less explain to anyone why he would even think of giving up his job to go to Chicago, hoping to get into a flying school that might not even accept him in the first place.

He came to two conclusions. The first was that his momma was right a long time ago when she had said that it was foolish for a black man to think about flying. The second was that as soon as his boss could find a replacement, he was going to take his foolish self to Chicago. He shook his head, laughed out loud, and climbed into his car for the drive back into Detroit.

A few days later a new limousine owned by a prominant black doctor stalled on the street in front of John's shop and could not be restarted. John walked out, introduced himself and offered to find and fix the problem.

He was quickly told by the doctor that "no one is to touch this car until my mechanic gets here."

With his formal degree in automotive technology, Robinson was not the least bit pleased by being turned down in favor of some mechanic from clear across town. He decided to hang around and see just who this favored craftsman might be.

It turned out to be Cornelius Coffey.

A meeting which began with a rather sarcastic Robinson and a somewhat indifferent Coffey ended with the discovery of a common interest in learning to fly. It was the beginning of a lifelong friendship.

# Chicago, 1927

One of John's traits was dependability. This led to his remaining some three months more at the garage in Detroit until a satisfactory replacement could be found. When he left, the garage owner gave him a letter of recommendation and a suggestion he was to follow.

"You have a complete set of tools, and I know you have saved your money. Why don't you look into opening your own small mechanics shop when you get to Chicago?"

Those friends who knew the real reason for his move to Chicago felt it was a crazy notion to follow. Among the most disappointed were several young ladies of the Detroit area who had set their sights on the quiet, confident mechanic.

The truth was that John was never really rash or foolish about anything. Determined, independent, and often stubborn, he was also possessed with enough common sense to temper his dreams by placing first things first.

In Chicago he took a room on the South side and transferred his savings to a local bank. He contacted several of his schoolmates from Tuskegee who lived in the area.

After two weeks of looking, he found a small building that had at one time been a combination hardware store and blacksmith shop. It needed some work but was suitable for conversion into a small mechanics shop. Besides, the rent was within the very tight budget John had to follow. For a while things were very slow. With the aid of his school friends and others he met in the neighborhood, a little business began to trickle into his shop. Most of his customers returned, for it was evident that this quiet young man from Mississippi knew what he was doing. Although he worked in a black area, within a few months white car owners, too, began coming to his shop. Robinson's Garage was going to make it.

The first few times he approached the Curtiss-Wright Aviation School he was turned down. They never said being black had anything to do with it. They were just filled up, or he had just missed the beginning of a new class, or try them in the spring, they told him.

John could hold his temper when he tried and he took the flying school's rejection with the determination to try again.

He gathered several friends from Tuskegee, and others he could interest, and formed an Aero Study Club. He did something else. He found that a weekend ground school was held at the Curtiss-Wright School, and he got a job, of all things, sweeping up the classrooms at night.

It seemed funny to him when he thought about it. "I told my daddy I had to leave the South to be able to use my education, that if I stayed, all I would get was 'sweeping jobs.' What if he knew that now I have a business of my own, I've gotten myself a job sweeping?"

But there was, as usual, method in his madness. He would close his shop, rush out to the Curtiss-Wright School, and quickly clean up all the rooms except the one the aviation ground school was being held in. Then he would spend the entire class period quietly dusting and sweeping in the back of the room. He listened to every word of instruction and discussion. After the class had left, or during coffee breaks, he would stay in order to copy the drawings and figures that had been left on the blackboard, into a small notebook. Of course, he did not do all of this without the knowledge and indeed the cooperation of the class instructor.

Sometimes the instructor would look to the back of the room and say, "You got that, Johnny, or are we moving too fast for you?"

Johnny would reply, "No, sir. I'm ambidextrous. I can move this broom and my mind at the same time."

On Sundays he would meet with his aero-study group and pass on the knowledge he gained while sweeping the back of the classroom at Curtiss-Wright. John decided that if he could not bring himself as a student to the school he would bring the school to himself.

John's friend, Cornelius Coffey, would often commute to Chicago to talk with Robinson about the possibilities of learning to fly. One way might be to build an airplane. John and Coffey pooled funds and purchased a kit from the Heath Parasol Airplane Company and a used motorcycle engine. The aero-study group now had a real project.

# But Will It Fly?

"What are you acting so worried about, Johnny? We almost have our plane ready to assemble and give it a try."

"Coffey, between you and me, that's exactly what I'm worried about. I started this thing as a way for us all to learn more about the mechanics of aviation, but I don't think I ever meant for us to really finish a whole aeroplane. I mean, we've all worked so hard, the group has a lot of pride in this thing; if this thing is finished and put together, hell, they gonna want to try it out. I don't know if I can find someone who will try to fly it, and even if I do, I don't know if I ought to ask him."

"Well, we've been doing things right, haven't we? I mean your figures check out, and the weight and all are right, aren't they? And hell, we've tried to make every part right."

"Yea, I believe all that, I'm proud of the job we've done, but trying to fly it, man, I got to tell you, it excites me, but it scares me too."

It excited a lot of people. Robinson and Coffey, in order to raise a little money and impress the ladies, displayed the aircraft at several big dances around town.

A few weeks later John told the whole story to Bill Henderson, the night class instructor at Curtiss-Wright. "Johnny, are you pulling my leg, or have you really built a plane?"

"Mr. Henderson, the group not only has built a plane, but plans to assemble it and take it out to a field this Sunday. They expect me to find them a flyer to try the thing out."

"Now wait a minute, John, I think I can guess what you have in mind and the answer is not just NO, but HELL NO!"

"Well, I just thought maybe you could come out and see the thing, sort of look it over and tell 'em what a good job they'd done and all, and then you and I could discuss some basic problem that the rest of us hadn't thought of to postpone the flight test until we go through a redesign. That would encourage the group and keep its interest up. Maybe the project would give me a better chance of getting accepted at the school. I'm not going to give up trying, anyway."

"John, you're crazy, in a quiet sort of way. You're smart and determined too. But the worst part is that I happen to like you, and damn if I don't believe you."

"It doesn't mean a damn thing except that I'll come out and look at the contraption, and that's all, you understand, that's all."

The afternoon was pleasant but dulled by a high overcast. The entire membership of the aviation study group was gathered around the small aircraft. They had been working on assembling their home-built aeroplane the entire Sunday morning. When they had finished, they filled the fuel tank and afterwards tied the plane's tail to a fence post.

Then, following John's instructions, they all took hold of the plane while John hand-propped the propeller. After several attempts, the motorcycle engine spit twice and sputtered into life. It scattered dust, loose grass, and several of the members of the study group. John got in the tight cockpit and checked the controls. Then he ran the engine up to full power. The plane tugged at the rope that held it to the fence. The prop was creating a surprising thrust to the tethered craft and it vibrated its protest from wing-tip to tail.

Satisfied, John shut the engine down and climbed out. In spite of himself, he could not hold back that Robinson smile.

"I want everything checked out one more time. Mr. Henderson should be here at two o'clock and it's one-thirty now."

Every member of the group knew each and every part of the small plane. They had cleaned, sanded, filled, drilled, sawed, primed, sewed, glued, and painted all the parts and pieces of the slab-sided little craft. They had worked out measurements, weights, lift and drag formulas, checking and rechecking every figure and every part.

Now they were all intent on doing one more thorough check of the plane. They also took turns sitting at the controls, as they had done a hundred times during the weekends and evenings they had spent building their flying project.

John was proud of the group and proud of the workmanship of the plane. He was also concerned. He had conceived the project, talked the group into trying to build it, and now that the members had indeed built an aeroplane he was worried about the outcome. They had learned so much by making a real aeroplane, and they longed to see it given the ultimate test.

Would it really fly? That's the part that worried him. That is why he had worked out the deal with Bill Henderson. John felt guilty about such an arrangement, but it was best, he thought, better than risking someone getting killed. That would do more damage to the interest of his group than not seeing its pet project get off the ground.

He also admitted to himself that he was responsible for the whole business. Though he wished he knew enough to try it himself, he didn't want to see anyone else risk his neck. Yet, he wanted to see it fly more than anyone else.

His thoughts were broken when someone shouted, "Here he comes. Here comes Mr. Henderson!" John could see the roadster turning in the gate in the fence and heading for the plane. "Well, here it comes," he said to himself.

They escorted Mr. Henderson to their pride and joy, the effort of many long volunteer hours of labor. He shook hands with John and then began a slow walk around the plane. He stopped to check a control, or a fitting, or the fabric on the wings. He studied the bracing wires, and gave a great deal of attention to the controls, the glued joints of the wooden fuselage and steel wing attachment fittings. Then he studied the engine installation, particularly the fuel line and electrical system and the engine mounts.

After about an hour of inspection he turned to Johnny. "This was your idea and you oversaw all the work on this bird?"

The group had been silent, except for answering occasional questions from Mr. Henderson. Now they gathered close around to hear the conversation. "Yes. I did some of the work, and all the people here had a hand in building it."

"Well, to tell you the truth, when you first told me about this project I really had my doubts. I expected to come out here and see some sort of crude kite, thrown together with more enthusiasm than mechanical skill. But I would like to tell you the workmanship, and in fact, the whole plane is not bad at all. I don't mind telling you, I'm surprised. It's not a bad looking little plane, all things considered. Would you mind if I got in and taxied it around the field?"

The group returned Henderson's smile, and several of them helped him into the cockpit. It was still tied to the fence. After the fuel tank was topped off, Henderson called for a start. "Switch off?" called Johnny. "Switch off," repeated Henderson. John swung the propeller through several times to prime the cylinders with fuel.

"Switch on, contact!" he called. "Contact," repeated Henderson, and he switched on the ignition. The warm engine caught on the first try and settled down into a steady idle. Bill Henderson motioned for the tail to be untied from the fence. He buckled his helmet chin strap. Johnny moved around to the cockpit yelling into Bill's ear, "I don't know about this, man. I thought you were going to find something conveniently wrong."

"So did I," answered Bill, "But I haven't found anything really wrong so far. Besides, I'm just going to make some taxi tests. I don't think that little motorcycle engine can get off the ground. How much fuel do I have?"

"You have six gallons, enough for about an hour and a half, and my figures show that that engine will get you airborne, but just barely, and that's the whole reason I'm worried. I mean don't you do anything foolish."

Bill looked at Johnny and said, "Look, I'm supposed to be the expert, remember. I'd be in a hell of a shape if I got hurt flying a contraption built by you African engineers, none of whom can even fly a plane himself."

"Yea," answered Johnny, "And I would have even less chance of ever getting into the flying school if I was responsible for getting one of their instructors killed. You remember this thing doesn't have any brakes, just the tail skid."

Bill studied the instruments on the small panel in front of him: a tachometer, an oil temperature gauge, and an altimeter. On the floor in front of the stick there was a large round compass of World War I vintage. Out on the wing strut he saw a wind-pressure, spring-calibrated, airspeed gauge. He nodded to John and the group around the plane.

Those holding the tail released their grip and the little plane moved out down the field as Bill Henderson eased in the throttle. He taxied the entire length of the field, turned around and taxied back toward the group, increasing the the plane's speed until he had its tail off the ground. As he neared the group he slowed down and turned around again.

This time he taxied at a good clip, turning slightly from side to side. Upon reaching the far end of the field he turned once again into the wind. John was the first to realize that the engine noise had changed and was now at full power. He stared down the field at the silhouette of the small plane coming at them head-on.

"Oh, Jesus, he's gonna do it!" he said quietly.

The engine now made a high whining sound as it spun the prop at full power. Still some distance away, the plane lifted momentarily into the air. Bill gently banked the plane from side to side testing the controls. The airspeed gauge crept past fifty-five miles per hour. Well before he reached the end of the field, Bill was sure the plane would fly, and he made his decision as the airspeed reached sixty.

"There he goes," shouted someone in the group. "Hot damn, he's flying!"

"God, Almighty, Johnny, we've done it. We made an aeroplane!"

And then it was up there, right over them. It wasn't exactly clawing its way into the sky, but it was flying, and it was theirs. With a laugh, John Robinson realized that he was probably the most amazed of all.

Henderson made a shallow bank and flew completely around the field waving as he once again came over the group.

He stayed within gliding distance of the field. Carefully, he eased the power back as he lined up for a landing. The plane tended to have a high-sink rate with the power all the way back to idle. He eased in a little power. Because he didn't trust the crude airspeed instrument he held a little extra speed. He was also careful to correct any wing drop using the rudder only, since he had not had the chance to test the stall characteristics of the little craft. He didn't want to chance stalling the wing, which at slow speed could be caused by too much, or by too sudden, a movement of the ailerons. A short flare, a bounce, and the flight was over.

Bill taxied up to a jubilant group of aeroplane builders, all of whom seemed determined to slap him on the back, pump his hand off, and ask more questions about the flight than he possibly could answer. Everyone was talking and shouting at the same time. Finally, Bill began to look around for Johnny, partly in desperation to get away from the crowd, which since all the group's friends and relations had come out for the big day, was about four times larger than the study group itself. He also wanted to congratulate John.

He saw him, arms folded across his chest, leaning against the fender of a roadster. As their eyes met, John broke into a wide grin and laughed, shaking his head from side to side in mock disbelief.

As Bill walked up to him, John reached into his back pocket, producing a pint of real bonded bourbon, a rare item during Prohibition. He held the bottle out to Henderson, "You said I was crazy when I told you we had built a flying machine, but you must be just as crazy 'cause you flew the thing."

Bill handed the bottle back to John, who took a sip and returned it to Henderson. Bill started to wipe the neck of the bottle off, then caught himself and glanced at Johnny who had not missed the gesture. Bill looked slightly embarrassed, then took a sip and looked straight at Johnny. "If a nigger can build an aeroplane," (Johnny's head snapped up in surprise, and Bill grinned), "then I guess I'll have to go back to Curtiss-Wright and convince them that a nigger can fly one." Then he took another swig of bourbon and handed the bottle to Johnny.

"I'll tell you what else. Maybe the group can donate the plane to the mechanical section of the school. It might lead to some openings in the mechanics school for some of the group. At least it would be a strong argument."

Other bottles began to appear among the crowd. From the assembled automobiles, baskets of chicken, potato salad, boiled eggs, ham, cake, and other goodies emerged from back seats and trunks.

It was a wonderfully happy evening. It ended when one of the group had to drive a very inebriated Henderson home. And someone not only had to drive Johnny home but he had to carry him to bed.

There was one more hurdle for John before he could join a flying class, as he learned a few days later from Bill Henderson.

"John, I've got to tell you that there is still more than a little opposition and skepticism with the powers that be at the school."

"But here is the good news along with the catch. The class beginning flight training next week has already finished ground school. The administration will let you join the class provided you can make a passing grade on the ground course exam between now and next Monday. Can you do it?"

"Well, I don't have much choice, now do I? Besides, I haven't been hanging around sweeping up the back of the classroom at night school just for sweeping money. I think I can do it."

"I think you can, too. One thing I didn't mention to the school was that you have been doing more than cleaning up the classrooms at night. If you do qualify, there are going to be a few people out there that are going to be surprised, and not everyone will be happy about it."

"And look, you are very likely going to get a rough introduction to flying by some of the guys who'll think they can give you more than you can take and then blame your quitting on your being colored. Do you get what I'm saying?"

"I've been gitten' it all my life from different members of the crowd, but I ain't quit yet. When I was a boy I thought things were a lot different in the North, and I guess opportunities are, but as far as true feelings, I find the North and the South aren't so different, except maybe the South is more honest about it. I know you have stuck your neck out for me, and I'm gonna do my best not to let either one of us down."

"O.K., Johnny, I guess that covers it."

"Not quite, Mr. Bill Henderson."

Bill turned back and Johnny said, "Thank you." Bill nodded, and took John's outstretched hand.

John passed the examination, scoring well on the mechanical portions, and was scheduled for flying instruction two afternoons a week. He also enrolled in the aircraft mechanics course. His garage business earned him enough money to pay the school and keep the bill collectors from his door—and feed him, provided he didn't tire of beans, bacon, potatoes, and once in a great while, a pork chop.

# A Twenty Dollar Bet

He reported early for his first flying lesson, and was sitting on a bench near the flight line watching a small plane making short circuits around the field practicing landings when Bill Henderson saw him and waved.

"John, it's a good day for your first lesson. The air is smooth, but remember what I told you. Your first flight or two won't be."

John believed him. His passing the exam had come as a surprise to the school's staff.

"They have never had a colored before," said Bill, "and some of the guys don't like it. I won't be your instructor, and you can bet whoever is will try to shake you up. Most think you will quit. Just hang in there. If you get sick, get sick, but if you really want to fly, hang in there and take it and you'll get through."

"I'll try too remember, Bill, I mean Mr. Henderson. I'm not gonna let you down."

"O.K. Johnny, I'll see you around."

Minutes later Johnny heard a voice behind him. "You have to be Robinson. I don't see any other nigger around here."

"That's right, I'm Robinson." He turned to face a large sandy-haired man he judged to be in his late thirties.

"My name is Johannsen and I drew you. I want you to know I didn't volunteer. You already know that no coloreds have ever been here to fly before. Some guys already think it's all going to be a big joke. They're wrong. I'm not a very funny guy. If business was slow I might have to put up with a poor student, but business is good and I don't turn out flybabies like a factory. I survived a war where I saw more so-called pilots killed by lack of flying ability than by the enemy. My students learn to be good pilots or I don't finish them through the school. I don't like clowns, and I won't be made a fool of. If you really want to be a pilot, I'll know that soon enough, and I'll make you one. But if you're out here just to make yourself the big nigger on Saturday night you better quit now, or go see if they'll give you another instructor. In the meantime, you'll call me Mr. Johannsen and if you have anything to say let's hear it now."

John was too angry and too hurt to reply. He shook his head from side to side to indicate he had nothing to say.

"All right, let's go check out the plane."

"Yes, sir," replied John, and followed the big Swede toward the bi-plane where they went over the preflight inspection to Johannsen's satisfaction.

"This is your helmet. You'll notice that it has tubes leading from the ear cups to this speaking tube. I can speak to you through them from the front cockpit. You do not have a speaking tube as there is nothing you have to tell me during flight. If I tell you to take the controls you will do so, signaling that you have the plane by wiggling the stick. If at anytime while you have the stick, I wiggle it, you will immediately release the stick to my control. Is everything clear up to now?"

"Yes, sir," replied Johnny.

"It better be. I had a student freeze up on the controls once. He damn near killed us both. You've passed the ground school test so I assume you know something about what makes a plane fly, and what the controls are for. Now crawl in the rear cockpit and let's go up and see what it's all about. We're going to take off, climb to four thousand feet, do some turns, some straight and level, and some stalls, in order to give you the feel of the aircraft in which you will be training. If during the stalls you get the plane in a spin, I'm going to give you the privilege of trying to get it out of the spin. If I wiggle the stick, or you feel me on the controls, let me take over. Now let's go."

Johannsen carefully checked to be sure John was securely fastened into his safety harness. He then climbed into the front cockpit and after fastening himself in, picked up the mouthpiece and called to Johnny, "The ground crew is ready to start the engine. I want you to call the signals to them."

The mechanic in front of the plane called out, "Off and closed."

John checked the magneto switch and pulled the throttle all the way back. "Off and closed," he replied.

The crewman turned the propeller through several times and called, "Brakes and contact!"

"Brakes and contact!" yelled John as he turned on the mag switch and pressed the heel brakes under the rudder pedals. The engine started on the first try and settled down to a syncopated rhythm, giving off the peculiar hot oil smell John had noticed in the Waco with Robert Williamson.

The faraway sound of Johannsen's voice coming from the rubber tubes into John's helmet instructed him to stay lightly on the controls through the taxi and takeoff. Johannsen taxied in a snakelike "S" course down the field which allowed them to see about ten degrees off on either side of the nose down the terrain ahead of them. John quickly learned that the pilot's view directly ahead is blocked by the nose of the aircraft as long as the tail remains on the ground. Only after the tail began to fly and was lifted during the takeoff roll was John able to see over the nose.

He would learn the same holds true for landings. The pilot flares the plane for landing, gradually pulling the stick back as the plane settles to earth. From that point until the plane slows down to taxi speed, the pilot of most tail-wheel planes can't see a thing ahead of him. He lands and rolls out looking off to either side of the landing area. Through experience John would gradually learn how to judge height above the ground, drift, and how to keep the plane rolling straight by looking to the side. All of this information came to John through the funny sounding voice from the speaking tube. He would soon become thoroughly accustomed to hearing that impatient voice from the little tube. The plane had hardly lifted from the ground when John felt the stick wiggle in his hand and heard the voice yell, "Climb to four hundred feet and turn to the left ninety degrees. Then climb to eight hundred and turn 45 degrees to the right, then climb straight up to 4,000 feet."

John took the controls and began a timid turn. "Use your rudder," said the voice. "Watch the nose, it's too high. Now it's too low." Each comment was followed by an unmistakably firm movement of the controls over-riding John's stiff and clumsy attempts. After a long period of too much up followed by too much down, John finally settled down to a more or less steady climb straight ahead.

John felt his self-confidence returning as he concentrated on making the climb smooth, keeping the plane's wings level and making only small corrections with the stick.

"Robinson, don't you think we could stop climbing now? We're at 5,500 feet! I told you to level off at 4,000 feet. Now ease off that throttle and get back down to 4,000. Don't dive, damn it, now you're climbing again. Get this thing in a glide and hold it straight." With much effort John found himself level at 4,000 feet at which point the voice called, "Turn to the right. Rudder, damn it, use the rudder!"

"Now turn left."

"Watch the nose!"

"Get that stick back!"

"Look at your air speed, for Christ's sake. You're supposed to be at 4,000 feet so get the hell back up there!" John was sweating and doing his own share of swearing, more at himself than at the voice that constantly battered his ears as he strained to hear its commands over the roar of the engine.

"Now we'll try a few stalls. You studied angle of attack and how the wing stalls if you get too great an angle, right?" John nodded to himself. "Now we're going to let you study one up close."

Johnny felt the stick move back as the plane changed into a nose-high attitude. "When you feel the nose begin to drop, remember to push the stick forward, give it gas, and keep the wings level with the rudder, until you get back your flying speed. You've got the aeroplane."

John felt it was the other way around but he held the stick back. The plane slowed its steep climb and began to shudder and buffet. Suddenly the right wing dropped, followed by the nose in a sickening descent that left John's stomach somewhere above, while his eyes stared down wildly at the earth.

His first reactions were all wrong. He jerked back on the stick, forgot to push in the throttle, and tried to pick the low wing up with the aileron. He felt a great desire to wet his pants.

The voice again: "Get that nose down, get this thing flying."

John pushed the stick forward toward the earth that was rising toward him. He held the stick there, then used the rudder to hold the wing level. Lo and behold, the airspeed began to build and he was flying again in a shallow dive.

"Now ease back and get us level." Much relieved for the moment, John found himself in a gentle straight flight. For the first time he looked out at the beautiful afternoon and the green fields below. His nervousness and tension were beginning to fade when the voice came at him again.

"O.K. Now let's climb back up and try a stall from a steep climbing turn, shall we?"

John's stomach, which had only just now caught up with him, tightened in a knot as he reluctantly eased the plane back to altitude. He found himself and the plane turning in a steep climbing bank to the left.

"When she breaks in the stall you will have the pleasure of attempting the recovery. This time, get the nose down."

When it broke into the stall John thought he would be ready—terrified, but ready—and he was. He got the stick forward, the power on, and managed to keep the plane from spinning. Let's go home now, he thought to himself. He felt worn out.

"O.K. That was better. Now let's go up and try one climbing to the right." John braced his nerve and started back up.

This time, just as the plane began to shudder in a steep climbing turn, Johannsen slammed the left rudder pedal forward. The plane whipped viciously over on its back as the nose dropped straight toward the earth which began spinning rapidly before the wide-eyed stare of the panic-stricken Robinson.

John shouted into the wind that now screamed by, and he felt himself being pressed down into his seat. His cheeks began to sag under the pressure. He barely heard the amazingly calm voice from the tube, saying "Rudder, damn it. We're in a spin. Use your right rudder and then the stick. You hear me, boy?"

The "boy" got through to him, and he heard his mind asking, "Nigger, you gonna be a nigger all your life?" John stomped on the right rudder and shoved the stick forward in fear and anger. At first nothing happened. Still they spun toward earth and panic clawed at him. But the rotation began to slow. Another turn and the plane stopped spinning. The airspeed increased. With shaking knees and hands John eased the plane back to level flight.

"All right," came the voice from the tube. "There's the field over to the left. I'll take it now. You follow me through on the landing."

John released what was still a death grip on the stick. His mouth was dry, he could feel the oncoming convulsions from his stomach. He leaned his head over the edge of the cockpit and vomited in mixed agony and relief. The spittle was sucked from his lips by the slipstream of air. It spread over his chin, cheeks and nose like rain over a windshield. He wiped his mouth with his sleeve and wiggled the stick to let Johannsen know he was still willing to fly. Johannsen let him fly until it was time for the landing.

He hardly remembered the landing. The silence as the engine shuddered to a stop snapped him back to attention and he struggled to get out of the cockpit. Johannsen was already standing on the ground when Johnny climbed down. His clothes were stained with sweat and vomit. John looked at his calm, neat instructor.

"Same time day after tomorrow, Robinson; that is, if you decide not to quit."

John looked at Johannsen. "I been wanting to fly all my life, and if I can't learn to fly because of you, Mr. Johannsen, then I'm gonna learn to fly in spite of you."

To John's surprise, he thought he detected a slight smile on the big Swede's face as he said, "You know, you just might at that. Now why don't you go get that bucket and rag over by the hangar and clean off the side of this aeroplane before anyone sees it. You're pretty much a mess, too. If you want to leave by the side gate I'll log you in. Next time, bring a paper bag with you."

"I won't need one any more. I'm gonna be a pilot."

Johannsen smiled, "Day after tomorrow, Robinson," he turned and left John alone with a very messy airplane. It didn't matter. John knew he would have his dream.

The young mechanic had intended to catch up on some of the work at his garage that evening but when he arrived home he was still feeling too sick and unsteady to work. He took the back stairs to his room. He wanted to avoid his friends who had been hanging around the shop to find out how his first flying lesson had gone. Still clothed, he lay down on his cot and stared up at the painted board ceiling.

He lay listening as voices argued in his mind. One kept telling him that flying couldn't be worth feeling so bad; that he wasn't going up there and go through that spinning misery; that they were deliberately making it hard and didn't want him, a black, to learn to fly, and maybe they were right.

Another voice broke through from time to time. It cried, "Yes, I can," and "Yes, I will," and at times, "Shut up, you chicken! You're going to learn to fly, damn it!" Finally, he drifted off to sleep, the voices quiet.

There had also been voices at the instructors' shack that afternoon. "Did you see that nigger cleaning off the side of the plane after his first lesson. Johannsen must have sure put him through it."

"Hell, that must have been them I saw spinning so damn far down this afternoon. For a minute I thought someone was out of control."

"If Johannsen put him through it, I don't think we'll

see any more nigger student pilots out here. Johannsen wasn't too happy when he drew him, you know."

"I'll bet twenty dollars the nigger never shows up for another lesson."

From a chair over in the corner Bill Henderson said, "I'll take ten dollars of that bet."

"Hell, Henderson, he's your nigger, but you're gonna lose your ten dollars. Anyone else want to cover the other ten dollars?"

"Yea, I'll take ten of that bet on Henderson's side."

The other instructors looked toward the door and saw Johannsen reaching in his hip pocket. "Here's my ten, Smitty," he said winking at Henderson as he turned, and walked off toward the flight line where his last student of the day was waiting.

The black student showed up for his next flying lesson as he did for all that followed. Johannsen, shouting instructions through the gasport tube, hammered out the rudiments of airmanship to the intensely determined Robinson. Near the end of his eighth hour of instruction, an hour that had been spent practicing endless circuits of touch-and-go landings, Johannsen motioned for Johnny to let him have the controls. He slipped the plane gently down to a landing, turned the plane around, taxied back to the end of the field and brought it to a stop, the engine ticking over slowly at idle.

John saw Johannsen unbuckle his safety harness and step from the plane. Believing something must be wrong, he rechecked the engine guages in his cockpit. He prided himself in his mechanical skills and was afraid he might be in trouble for having missed the problem that had obviously caused his instructor to take control of the plane and land it.

He was still looking down at the cockpit instruments, trying to hear or feel whether something was amiss with

the smoothly idling engine when he heard the obviously
impatient voice of his instructor.

"Well, Robinson, what are you waiting for?" John
looked at him with a blank expression. "You going to sit
there all day confusing everyone who wants to land here,
or are you going to fly that thing?" John's blank face
changed to startled discovery.

"Now remember, Johnny, do just what you have been
doing all afternoon. I want you to take off, come around
for one touch-and-go and then right back here for a full
landing to pick me up. Don't leave the field, and remember to watch for other aircraft. Now you got that?"

"Yes, sir." John stared for a second at his instructor
walking away from the plane. The front cockpit was
empty for the first time.

He became aware that his palms were getting sweaty.
As he looked around at the airplane in which he now sat
alone, he had a flash of fear and of self-doubt. The peculiar thought that the plane was alive like some animal
came into his mind. He recalled his mother telling him
he had no business "fooling around with a flying machine." He thought he heard a jeering voice calling out,
"the white bossman is leaving you, boy, and his animal
is gonna git you."

He wiped his hands on the knees of his britches and
carefully went through the simple checkout of the engine
and controls.

Satisfied that no other plane was in the landing pattern
he glanced around to look for Johannsen, who stood
relieving himself near the edge of the field, legs apart,
his back toward Johnny.

"Well, hell!" John said to himself and eased the throttle
to full power. All his thoughts were concentrated on
making a smooth takeoff. It was not until the wheel had
stopped bouncing after leaving the ground that John

Robinson's serious face suddenly changed to shining joy as he rolled gracefully into a gentle turn.

"God Almightly, I'm flying!" He whooped and shouted and reached out into the slipstream. John beat his hands on the side of the plane as if to make it climb faster.

He filled his senses with the moment—the sounds, the smells, the rush of air, the beauty of the earth spread out below him. It was a moment of exhilaration that would stay in his memory forever—his first solo flight.

His landings were not good but it did not matter. He had flown alone and the self-confidence born in that act would aid in smoothing out his novice technique, as Johannsen well knew.

"All right, Robinson, now that we've got that over with maybe you can settle down and learn how to fly an airplane. If you think the undercarriage won't collapse on us after those two horrible landings, taxi back to the flight shack and I'll buy you a cup of coffee."

"Yes, sir." John tried to look serious, but he could not stop grinning for two days. There was something else. Back at the coffee shack he got hand shakes and congratulations, and in the weeks that followed he no longer had to wait alone, without friends or greetings, for his turn on the flight line.

The days at Curtiss-Wright were wonderful beyond his hopes. He not only qualified as a licensed pilot but continued his training, learning aerobatics, and qualifying in all the aircraft available at the school including multiengined craft such as the Ford trimotor. He so impressed the school with his mechanical ability and his marks in aviation mechanics that he was offered a job with Curtiss-Wright as a mechanical instructor.

These were no small accomplishments for a young man, especially a young black man. Yet he retained his modest demeanor. Instead of using his accomplishments to set himself apart, John Robinson continued to share his knowledge with his friends, encouraged those around him. He enjoyed sharing his dream. He didn't forget his friend Coffey who was accepted for flying school.

Robinson pioneered by interesting an entire class of black students, including several girls, in enrolling in the Curtiss-Wright aviation mechanics school. Because the flying facilities of the school were not "available" for this group, John Robinson called upon the leaders of Robbins, Illinois, an all-Negro town near Chicago. With their help, he established America's first airfield completely owned and operated by Negroes, and founded the Challenger Air Pilots Association.

Robinson's energy and enthusiasm seemed limitless. He taught at Curtiss-Wright, and set up the first Negro flying classes given to blacks in America, at the first all-Negro airfield which he'd helped found. Yet he found time to pursue his own advancement in flying, earning a commercial multi-engine aviation transport license.

# Hummingbird

Robinson got his pilot's license in 1927. Coffey got his in 1928. They both knew there were many blacks who wanted to learn to fly. They also knew better than anyone else that no flying school would readily accept black students.

John decided to provide one. The question was how? He didn't have much money. A flying school had to have a plane.

There was a used car salesman named Abbott who advertised that he had an aeroplane for sale he had taken in on trade. John Robinson knew a thing or two about trading and automobiles.

Abbott, a pilot himself, did not expect a black to reply to his ad and he did not at first take John seriously. But, as with everything else concerning aviation, John was persistent.

John had a Hudson Sedan that he had rebuilt. He took it and Cornelius Coffey to see Abbott. Abbott said the car was nice but not enough, John said, "O.K., how much more?"

Abbott said, "How much you boys have?" John didn't have any money. Coffey had two hundred dollars. Robinson said, "The car and two hundred dollars, and you give each of us a three hour check out in the plane."

"I don't know," said Abbott.

"Hell," said Robinson, "who else would buy an off-brand aeroplane as ugly as that one?"

Abbott scratched his head, walked up and down a few minutes and said, "O.K., give me the car keys and the two hundred bucks."

The plane ironically was called a White Hummingbird and was painted black. It had a World War I OX5 engine. The open cockpit bi-plane would seat two in front and the pilot in the back. It was slow, a handful to get out of a spin, which it was prone to do if handled sloppily, but it flew. Robinson and Coffey had their first plane and their first partnership together. The John Robinson School of Aviation was soon to follow.

One of the first students to apply to the John Robinson School of Aviation was a nineteen-year-old named Harold Hurd, who already knew the basics of flying. Before John opened the school, Hurd, by his persistence had talked a white flying instructor at Midway airport into giving him flying lessons. However, the only time the lessons were available was at five-thirty in the morning at first light. That way no one was likely to know the instructor was giving lessons to a black. The instructor, although taking Hurd's money for lessons, refused to solo him, arguing that "it would be bad for business."

When Johnny Robinson met Harold Hurd, he took an immediate liking to him and, in turn, Hurd looked upon Robinson almost as a "big brother." Robinson allowed Hurd to "tag along with him" in the air as well as on the ground. Harold once heard one of Johnny's girlfriends complain, "Why do you always have to bring that kid along?"

On one occasion when Hurd was flying under Robinson's supervision, an incident occurred which illustrates the problems of blacks involved in aviation during the early 1930s. At the time Robbins airfield did not have fuel facilities. Robinson agreed to let Hurd fly him in an International OX5 bi-plane for a short flight. The OX5 had only a third of a tank of fuel when they took off. Although there was enough fuel to return to Robbins field, they decided to fly to Ashburn field which had fuel available. (Ashburn was the oldest airfield in Chicago, often visited by Lindbergh and other great aviators of the day). After landing they taxied up to the fuel pump. When the attendant came out ankd discovered the flyers were black, he informed them in no uncertain terms that Ashburn field was closed to coloreds. He flatly refused to sell them any gasoline.

Now dangerously low on fuel, they had little choice but to take off from Ashburn field as quickly as possible since the ground crew was hostile. They barely managed to reach Midway Airport where they were allowed to purchase fuel.

Such examples of the difficulties encountered by blacks determined to fly make it easy to understand the early success of the J. C. Robinson School of Aviation.

Unknowingly, John had quietly begun building in the 1930s the legacy that would help carry black flyers into space fifty years later.

# Tall Tree—Short Cotton

Robinson became a professional pilot during the "Golden Age of Aviation", which unfolded in the rapidly changing world of the twenties and thirties. Lindbergh had soloed the Atlantic; new records in aviation were being made daily; air races, stunt flying, and the rapid advancement of aircraft design were all making the front pages of the nation's newspapers. Doolittle, using Sperry's new gyro instruments, had successfully taken off in a plane with a hood, flown a course, and landed. Blind to the world outside his cockpit, he had referred only to the aircraft's instruments. Air travel was becoming more acceptable to the public. John Robinson, believing there was a place for Negro youths in aviation, searched for better facilities in which to teach them. He also believed the best way to lead was by example and hard work, and he searched for meaningful ways to teach these principles. A changing world was to offer him both chances, but timing would require him to choose which path to follow first; events would not allow him to do both simultaneously.

The roaring twenties had rushed full throttle to their disastrous end, plunging the world's economies into depression. Though aviation suffered serious setbacks, the stronger companies held on. One of those was Curtiss-Wright which counted among its employees a black pilot and aviation mechanic. To John the Depression was just another problem he had to overcome in his determination to keep aviation as his career and to also create opportunities for other blacks. This determination would endanger him.

There were two other men of dreams whose paths he would cross. One was a school dropout, an atheist, a former corporal in World War I, and a Fascist who had strong-armed his way to power and now dreamed of conquest. The other was the regent of an ancient Christian nation. This man dreamed of bringing his people into the modern world. Among other tasks, he struggled to persuade his nation to abolish slavery.

The winds of war were blowing once more and the first squalls of what was to be a decade of war storms were gathering over the plateaus of Ethiopia—blown across Africa from the streets of Rome.

Benito Mussolini, "Il Duce", had come to power by forcefully using his Fascist militia in 1922 and by promising to bring the "Glories of Rome" once again to Italy.

Having the total power of a dictator, he did much to modernize Italy, beginning with her war machinery. But Il Duce's spending added monetary stress to the nation. The world depression was now threatening to collapse Italy's economy and Mussolini along with it. He had promised a new Italian empire, he had built a war machine at great expense, and he needed to fulfill his promise.

What better place to begin than with a backward African nation, assumed to contain unexploited natural resources? Backward or not, Ethiopia had given the Italians an embarrassing defeat at Adowa in 1896. The conquest of Ethiopia would revenge that defeat and add to the "glory of the Italian empire." It would provide land for the badly crowded citizenry of Italy to colonize and would benefit their sagging economy. So many of the tactics attributed to Hitler, which would shock the world in 1939, were openly conceived and displayed with pomp by Mussolini in 1935. That few in the world paid any attention, proved not only sad but terribly costly.

In 1930, upon the death of Empress Zauditu, her cousin, Ras Tafari, who had served as regent, became em-

peror of Ethiopia. He assumed the name Haile Selassie
(Power of the Trinity), Neguse Neguse (King of Kings),
Elect of God and Conquering Lion of Judah. He had been
educated in England and after his coronation, opened
the doors to Western influence. His nation comprised
five or more different peoples and numerous tribes. At
least four major languages were spoken in Ethiopia.
There were few schools. His country had never been fully
mapped and had never had a nationwide census. Slavery
was common, the highland Ethiopians often raided the
Negroid Abigars and Annuaks of the Sudan area for
manpower.

The new emperor took on the enormous task of bringing his nation into the twentieth century. He worked
toward abolishing slavery. Ethiopia joined the League
of Nations in 1923. As Emperor, Haile Selassie, implemented a new constitution which set up two houses of
parliament. He appointed the members of the senate
while the provincial leaders chose the members of the
chamber of deputies. These were difficult changes for a
nation that had chosen Christianity in the fourth century
A.D. and had been isolated by the rise of Islam in the
seventh century A.D. (It was the only country in North
Africa not to fall before Islamic swords). His Imperial
Majesty, Haile Selassie was determined to bring his
country into the twentieth century. This man of small
physical stature grew tall in world respect.

Italy controlled Eritrea on Abyssinia's (Ethiopia's)
northern border and Italian Somaliland on its southeast-
ern border. Because the borders had long been undemar-
cated Mussolini thought it would be easy to provoke
border incidents sufficient to bait Ethiopia into commit-
ting a retaliatory border incident that he could use as an
excuse for war (the same tactic Hitler would later use
against Poland).

Italian Marshall Emilio de Bono and Benito Mussolini had agreed to engage in a war with Ethiopia and began preparations as early as 1933. In 1934 Bono sent a telegram to Mussolini saying Haile Selassie would not attack and the war must be started by Italy. Emperor Haile Selassie, instead of resorting to arms, made a noble and sincere plea to the League of Nations in an attempt to save his country from a senseless war. Though its eloquence was long remembered, the plea was in vain.

In the United States of the thirties, there was great interest among American blacks in the leader of the oldest black empire in the world. Ras Tafari, Christian Ruler, was descendant of a ruling family which traced its roots to Menelik the First, the legendary child of King Solomon and Queen Sheba. Ras Tafari became the object of adoration among American blacks. Groups of his admirers called Tafariests were popular. Their interest was reflected in the Negro press, especially that of the larger cities such as New York, Chicago, and Detroit.

John Robinson, though aware of world events, was caught up in the unfolding success of his own dreams. In his search for better facilities in which to involve blacks in the field of aviation, he took the natural course of turning toward his old school, the Tuskegee Institute. His inquiry to school officials in 1934 brought an invitation to return to his alma mater on the tenth anniversary of his class' graduation to discuss his suggestion. He accepted the invitation.

John invited his partner Cornelius Coffey and Grover C. Nash, a black pilot Robinson had helped teach to fly, to make the flight to Tuskegee with him.

However, Robinson didn't have a plane available for the flight because the school plane was scheduled for use by students. Grover Nash had a small midwing Buhl Pup monoplane with a three cylinder radial engine but it had only one seat. They would have to have a second plane.

Needing a two-place plane to fly Coffey and himself to Tuskegee, John persuaded Janet Waterford, one of his former flying students who had purchased an OX5 bi-plane, in the Chicago Challenger Air Pilot's Association to loan him her plane. Ms. Waterford was a registered nurse. She and John Robinson had become very good friends. It was no secret that John Robinson was fond of attractive ladies. But this attractive lady could not only fly, she owned a beautiful bi-plane. In 1934 that was extraordinary.

John wanted to arrive at Tuskegee with two aircraft and two of his former students, Coffey, an instructor and his partner in Chicago, and Nash, a licensed pilot. Robinson was determined to show the viability of a black school of aviation at Tuskegee.

The flight took careful planning. Gordon Nash's little Buhl Pup carried only seven gallons of fuel. Despite the small three cylinder engine, the plane's range was short and would require frequent stops for refueling. In 1934 there were far fewer airfields that could provide fuel than can be found today. The OX5 Robinson and Coffey were flying had a fifty gallon fuel tank and considerably more range.

The flight went well until they left Murpheesboro, Tennessee heading towards Birmingham, Alabama. On this leg of the flight they encountered strong headwinds. Nash signaled (by pointing to his gas tank) that he was very low on fuel. They searched their maps as well as the ground below for an airfield within close range.

Near Decatur in Alabama, Nash signaled he had to go down and immediately began to descend toward the only available landing area—the Decatur Golf Course. The fairway was smooth and flat but very short. Nash landed with only a few drops of fuel left in his tank. Robinson, who had circled above while Nash landed, now brought the OX5 around and slipped it nicely onto the smooth but short fairway.

To say that the few golfers out that day were surprised is hardly adequate. Not one, but two aeroplanes had landed right on the number six fairway! If the golfers were astonished at seeing two planes land, they were utterly amazed when three black pilots climbed down from the cockpits! No less awed were the Negro caddies who worked at the all-white country club.

The only voice heard was that of an irate sportsman who demanded that his opponent allow him a free shot since he had putted his ball from the sixth green clear onto the next fairway when the landing aircraft had, as he put it, "nearly taken my head off!"

It was such an unusual event that a friendly atmosphere developed and a volunteer phoned from the club-house for a gas truck.

"How much fuel do you need?" asked the voice on the end of the line.

The fairway upon which they had landed was of minimum takeoff length. In addition, on the far side of the fence just at the end of the fairway stood a row of sharecroppers' cabins. Beyond the cabins there stretched a cotton field.

Robinson had decided to refuel only the little Buhl Pup because the OX5 had enough gasoline to reach Birmingham.

"Tell him seven gallons."

"He says he can't afford to deliver less than twenty-five gallons all the way out here from town."

"O.K.," John said. He had no other choice.

1934 was the depth of the Great Depression. Money was not wasted by anyone, and certainly not by a struggling black flying partnership. At least that is how John saw it. When, after paying for the twenty-five gallons, he was asked what to do with the remaining eight-

een, John said, "Don't waste it. Go ahead and put it in
the OX5."

Coffey was a very conservative flyer. He usually went
along with John's decisions out of respect for the latter's
greater experience. On this occasion, however, Coffey
disagreed. The extra eighteen gallons of fuel would add
over a hundred pounds of weight to the OX5. He didn't
want that extra weight when they would have to take off
from such a short field.

Robinson said they could make it and began a preflight
check of the plane. Coffey, still unconvinced, picked up
a stick and walked off some distance down the field to a
point where he figured a takeoff run could safely be
aborted in case it was necessary. He thought that at that
point there still could be enough room to stop before
reaching the fence separating the golf club from the
sharecroppers' homes. He tied his handkerchief to the
stick and stuck it in the ground as a marker.

Grover Nash was already in the air, having taken off
in the light Buhl Pup with no difficulty. Using all the
space available on the fairway, Robinson, flying from the
back seat began the takeoff roll in the OX5. Coffey, sitting
in the front cockpit leaned his head to the left to look for
the marker he had placed further down the field. John
got the tail up and the controls began to feel light to his
touch.

"No sweat" he thought to himself, "she's going to fly
us out of here." He was committed to the takeoff. At the
same time, Coffey saw his marker fly by just as the OX5
lifted off the ground. Coffey reached for the throttle and
closed it.

Startled, John immediately rammed the throttle open.
The OX5 momentarily lost altitude until full power was
restored and then slowly began to climb. They had
crossed the fence, the row of cabins with their brick
chimneys was just ahead.

Both John and Cornelius thought they had made it. Then they heard as well as felt a sharp bump. Robinson concentrated on flying the plane. A very distinct vibration had developed in the controls. Coffey thought that the landing gear must have struck a rooftop. He unfastened his seat belt and, holding the cabane struts, leaned forward out of the cockpit to look down at the wheels. They seemed all right. Then he looked back past John to the tail. Half of the horizontal stabilizer was gone, torn off by one of the brick chimneys! While he turned to refasten his seatbelt, Coffey motioned for Johnny to look back at the tail. Coffey wasn't too worried about landing in the huge cotton field until he looked forward. Dead ahead was one oak tree standing in the center of the field!

This time it was John who closed the throttle. He wanted to get the plane down before the entire tail came off. He wasn't at all concerned about landing in the cotton field. From the back seat he couldn't yet see the oak tree!

Startled when John cut the throttle, Coffey, staring at the very leaves of the tree as the plane's nose dropped, shoved the throttle forward. He grabbed the stick in an effort to bank the plane away from the tree. John, now aware of the tree was already taking evasive action. It was too late.

They had almost made it, but only a few feet off the dry sunbaked cotton field, a wingtip caught a low branch of the tree.

Circling above in the Pup Grover Nash watched in horror as the OX5 spun around and crashed tail first into the field. It caused a huge grey explosion that grew into a cloud obscuring the plane and its crew from his view. Nash, flying low above the frightening scene, was sure that the plane's fuel tank had exploded and killed his friends. A few moments later, however, he was astonished to see both Robinson and Coffey walk out of the grey cloud and wave up at him.

As the dust settled, Nash realized that there had been no explosion. The frightening cloud had just been an enormous swirl of dust thrown up as the plane crashed into the drought-stricken cotton field. Nash caught sight of what remained of Janet Waterford's OX5—a wingless, tailess heap of debris.

Robinson and Coffey were furious with one another because of their mixed-up signals but by the time Nash landed they had decided not to kill each other. They calmed down enough to realize that they both had made mistakes and they should simply be satisfied to be alive.

As Nash walked up, the two survivors were arguing about a far more serious matter.

"You call her." Nash heard one say. "You call her, you are the one who pulled the throttle on takeoff," said the other. Nash convinced them to flip a coin. Coffey won the honor of calling Janet Waterford and telling her they had just scattered her bi-plane all over central Alabama. She was not amused.

But there was one item that they did not argue about. The important thing was for them to pursue John's goal of establishing a school of aviation at Tuskegee. It was decided that John would fly on to Tuskegee in the Buhl Pup while Coffey and Nash salvaged the engine from the destroyed OX5.

It was a beautiful Alabama spring day as the sound of an aircraft caused eyes to look skyward over the campus of Tuskegee. John circled low over the buildings and then made several passes over a field on the campus farm. Captain A. J. Neeley, the registrar at the college, accompanied by other members of the faculty and a large portion of the student body, had gathered at the field earlier. John set the plane onto the thick grass and taxied toward the waiting crowd. It was a midwinged wire-braced monoplane. When the helmeted and parachute-attired Robinson climbed from the open cockpit, he was somewhat embarrassed by the applause from the crowd. In all honesty, he had been so quiet and serious a student that only a few of his fellow classmates and his teachers remembered him.

But on this occasion he was Tuskegee's intrepid aviator and was indeed welcomed home. He enjoyed the festivities but wasted no time in discussing with President F. D. Patterson the possibility of establishing a genuine Negro school of aviation at Tuskegee. Before he left to return to Chicago, not only had he sold the idea of a school of aviation, but he had also been engaged to head the department, beginning the following fall term.

Feeling a sense of achievement and happiness, he found the sky brighter and the earth greener as he flew toward Chicago. With an occasional roll or loop, he danced with the clouds. It was his sky that day.

He sent the news to his parents and his sister, who was a teacher, too. He then informed Curtiss-Wright and Coffey, his partner, of his plans. The press began to seek him out for interviews.

His small part of the world was all right. Unfortunately, the rest of the world was not.

Many pilots will agree that an aircraft will almost always give indications of oncoming problems such as oil leaks, subtle noises or vibrations, in time to allow the prudent pilot to avoid catastrophe. Unlike well-trained aviators, those in high places who pilot the world almost always seem unwilling or unable to take corrective action in time to prevent disaster. By 1935 the world faced a decade of war in all its modern horror, and it was to begin in Ethiopia.

Border "incidents" increased. News stories around the world made it plain throughout 1934 that Mussolini intended to use them as an excuse for a military action in Ethiopia. After several clashes of armed patrols along the border of Italian Somaliland near Walwalth Ethiopia, Haile Selassie appealed to the League of Nations, asking it to send neutral observers and to take on the arbitration of the border incidents. The League refused and locked itself into non-action. Mussolini sent large numbers of troops and arms to Africa, stating in the world press that Italy had a "civilizing mission" in "backward" Ethiopia.

Italy voiced the sentiment that the Ethiopian victory in 1896 over Italian troops at Adowa had to be avenged. Mussolini announced his intention to annex the lowlands of eastern Ethiopia, permitting the expansion of a "Fascist empire" through the "glory of Italian arms." At the same time the world listened to the impassioned plea of Haile Selassie as he appeared before the assembly of the League of Nations. He asked for peace, withdrawing his troops from the disputed borders to prevent any further border incidents. Though England was anti-Italian, she refused to pledge aid in the event of war. France's response also was cold. When the Italian delegation walked out of the assembly, the League of Nations did nothing.

There was full coverage of Haile Selassie's plea in the American press. Many groups, especially among blacks, formed societies to send aid to Ethiopia.

Although John Robinson was not involved in any of these groups directly, his admiration for Haile Selassie had grown as a result of the intense news coverage given the developing threat of war in Ethiopia.

John's life had seemed very much in order with the challenge of heading a new department at Tuskegee. Now the idea of a new challenge began to form in his mind. Not only did he feel the school was needed to train black youth in aviation-related skills, but he knew to be accepted as pilots and aircraft mechanics blacks needed an opportunity to prove by example that they could excel in aviation. This had not yet been done. There had been few other black pilots. Among them was Hubert Julian, who claimed to be the first black parachutist and the first black licensed pilot.

John felt Julian had not necessarily set a proper example, judging him to be less of a serious aviator than a promoter of moneymaking schemes sometimes bordering on fraud.

Julian had parachuted into Manhattan as a stunt. He had collected funds "among the patrons of flying and fans of The Black Eagle," the name he had taken for himself, for a proposed solo flight to Ethiopia from Harlem. In a single-engined float plane he planned to fly to Ethiopia via Florida, the Caribbean, and South America. Finding few backers he appealed to the public through advertising. He was informed by an agent of the U.S. Government that he had better make the flight because there was a law against collecting funds through the mail with intent to defraud.

With much fanfare Julian took off from the Harlem River on his African flight. The flight lasted about five minutes, ending in a crash into Flushing Bay. Though it was not the sort of example John Robinson knew black aviation needed, the news of the attempt somehow reached the emperor of Ethiopia who was impressed by the idea of black pilots. Ethiopia's small air fleet was flown by French pilots. The emperor wanted to prove to his people that black men could indeed learn to fly, an idea that was not encouraged by his French pilots. Julian, "The Black Eagle," was happy to accept the emperor's invitation and traveled to Ethiopia to demonstrate his flying ability. Upon his arrival he was given rank, a uniform, living quarters, and much attention. He did demonstrate to the emperor's pleasure—and to the consternation of the French pilots—that a black could indeed fly, but he overdid things. Some months later during a celebration, he disobeyed the orders of the emperor. While still regent, Haile Selassie had been given a prized gift from a London firm—a sporty little white deHavilland Gypsy Moth bi-plane. Haile Selassie had given orders that no one was to fly it until his coronation. During national festivities it was usually put on display for the crowds. On one particular occasion, to the dismay of the regent's aide and to the surprise of Haile Selassie, Julian took off in the sparkling white craft and began to show off directly over the airstrip in front of the viewing stand. He stalled the plane which entered a spin and crashed into the top of a eucalyptus tree. The next day Julian was expelled from Ethiopia and the *New York Times* carried the story of the Black Eagle of Harlem being ordered out of the country in disgrace. There was some talk suggesting Julian had barely escaped being fed to the royal lions.

Robinson viewed Julian's misadventures with anger and dismay. The news media had played Julian's so-called attempted African flight with comic sarcasm and after his misadventure gleefully announced: "American Negro Pilot Flies Emperor's Plane into Eucalyptus Tree."

John knew what those kinds of stories did to attempts to open aviation to blacks. He longed for an opportunity to demonstrate a black pilot's abilities in a way that would gain favorable publicity in the press and acceptance by the aviation community. Now, if war came to Ethiopia, such an opportunity might be available. If so, it would conflict with his opening the school of aviation at Tuskegee for which he had worked so hard. During the months that followed, he worked toward preparing for the move to Tuskegee, but he knew a conflict of opportunity and decision lay in the road ahead, and he would have to make up his mind.

Despite his quiet manner, John's steady progress in aviation and his demonstrated ability stirred the interest of the press in his activities. Now that he had been presented the opportunity to establish an department of aviation at Tuskegee Institute, he found himself the object of interviews and invitations to meet with leaders of business and education.

At one such meeting sponsored by the Associated Negro Press, John voiced for the first time a conviction that had been growing stronger in his mind. He confided to the assembled group of executives that the cause of aiding blacks to enter the field of aviation might best be served by a black aviator's example of professional ability. He suggested that the apparent situation in Ethiopia might provide such an opportunity, stating that he would like to go there and offer his services.

One of the executives present, Claude Barnett, was the friend of the nephew of Emperor Haile Selassie, Dr. Halaku Bayen, who was in the United States at the time. Barnett went to Washington for a conference with the Ethiopian princeling and discussed with him the conversation he had had with John Robinson.

Bayen met with John to determine his sincerity and professional flying proficiency. Satisfied with Robinson's response, Bayen forwarded a report to Addis Ababa.

In spite of Ethiopia's urgent need for skilled technical personnel, the emperor, remembering the unfortunate earlier experience with another black American pilot, Hubert Julian, received the report with serious reservations. However, Robinson had such an impeccable set of references that Emperor Selassie cabled John, warmly inviting him to accept a commission in the Ethiopian army.

# The Lonely Voyage

On a late afternoon in May of 1935 on the deck of an outward-bound steamship, passengers lined the rail watching the lighted skyline of New York descend below the horizon. Among them, standing alone, hands in his pockets, was a slim brown-skinned young man. He was thinking of his mother in Gulfport, Mississippi, and of her distress that instead of accepting a teaching position at Tuskegee, he was going halfway round the world to a strange nation that was apparently headed for war.

His family had pleaded with him not to go. John's relatives couldn't accept his belief that he could advance the opportunities of blacks at home more by going to Ethiopia than by teaching at Tuskegee.

The chilled evening breeze smelled of the sea, a familiar smell of his childhood on the Gulf Coast. John thought of his mother's seafood gumbo and how far away those days now seemed. Opportunities, decisions —was he choosing or being chosen, or just being swept along? He left the rail and walked toward the main dining salon. "Well," he thought to himself, "I might feel a little unsure and lonely about leaving the States for the first time but I'm sure doing it in style."

It was true. Dr. Bayen had booked first-class passage for him and had made all the necessary arrangements for his trip. He'd helped John secure a passport and had provided ample cash for the voyage. In filling out the passport application, John had to state a reason for his traveling to Ethiopia. He listed business, claiming that he was planning to sell aircraft to the Ethiopian Government. He certainly could not say that he expected to become a member of the Ethiopian air corps since it is against the law for an American citizen to serve in the Armed Forces of another government, particularly one at war. But John felt pretty sure he would wind up in exactly those circumstances.

He scratched his shoulder where his vaccination for smallpox still itched, and followed a waiter to his seat in the lavishly decorated dining salon. He was aware of a few curious glances by some at his table, but, as a rule, his fellow diners were polite. They were also intrigued by him. During the first leg of the trip from New York to Marseilles, the rumor that he was a pilot and a soldier of fortune had increased their curiosity. To his embarrassment he became somewhat of a celebrity on the ship. There were also some who made no secret of their distaste for booking first class passage only to find "a damn Chicago nigga" enjoying the same privileges.

A group of German businessmen did not miss the opportunity to discuss the Nazi theory of a superior race one evening when they were sure he could overhear. Most of the passengers were American vacationers of the "old money" set, the class that is usually the least hurt by monetary depression and which generally, is the last to change life styles. Among them was a former pilot who had flown with the 94th Aero Squadron in the Great War. He approached John on the third afternoon of the crossing.

"Robinson, I hear you've done a little flying. Is that true?"

John replied, "That's right, I've done a little."

"Heard you were from Chicago, but you don't sound like a native of the Windy City."

"I was raised on the coast of Mississippi. You don't sound like a Northerner yourself."

"No. I'm from the Carolina coast—Charleston. Is it true you are headed for Ethiopia and the mess that's fixing to happen over there?"

"Yes, that's where I'm going."

"I made the same mistake in 1917, but no one could talk me out of going at the time. I suppose you've been told you're crazy enough times already. Why don't you and I go to the bar and talk flying. I'm damn tired of bridge, my children are driving me crazy, and my wife is seasick in her cabin, or says she is. I haven't done any flying for a while. I'm forty-one and I'm supposed to be wiser, but I miss it."

The two spent much of the remainder of the crossing walking the decks and exchanging stories about flying. The Carolinan said he had spent most of the war running like crazy since he had been assigned to fly a slow, lumbering observation plane that seemed to be the prey of every German birdman.

"Man, did I love the clouds. I'd run for cover if a cloud was near. Once inside I couldn't tell up from down, and many a time I would spin out of the bottom, sick as hell, but I stayed alive, and got my observer and the messages through most of the time. I finally got assigned to a fighter squadron and thought I was lucky, but hell, I had more close calls in fighters than before. It really wasn't much fun, John, the war, I mean, but I miss the flying."

John learned from the veteran's knowledge of air tactics. He enjoyed the company and the shared laughter. In his cabin at night he knew he needed a little laughter and company, for when he was alone in the darkness, self-doubt would creep into his mind. And the miles separating him from home and all those he knew grew in pace with the slow rhythm of the ship's engine, only faintly detectable in his first-class stateroom.

After his arrival in France he spent three glorious days in Paris, later departing from Marseilles on a smaller steamer to continue his seven-thousand-mile journey. He crossed the Mediterranean, traveled down the Suez Canal, across the Red Sea and then through the straits of Bab al Mandab into the Gulf of Aden, finally arriving at the port of Djibouti, the capital of French Somaliland.

The port teemed with activity. Small, ancient sailing craft loaded with trading goods crowded the shore. Laborers swarmed about unloading the few steamers in the harbor, where the tricolor flag of France flew over the customs building.

"Mr. Robinson?" John turned to face a bearded black man with high cheek bones and sharply defined facial features. He spoke English with a distinct British accent. "I am honored to have the privilege of escorting you to Addis Ababa. All arrangements have been made and we will leave by train in the morning. I know you must be tired. Your dinner and your room at the hotel are waiting. We will have ample time for a briefing and all your questions during the train trip."

John thanked the envoy. After making polite conversation during dinner, he gladly found his way to his quarters and attempted to sleep, surrounded by the sweltering heat of the tropical evening, and the exotic sounds and smells of Djibouti. Still awake after an hour, he opened a bottle of French wine and read through a copy of the *London Times* he had bought in the lobby. It was over three weeks old. He skimmed over the article concerning Italy's official protest over the sale of American arms to Ethiopia and the country's announcement that as a result of this sale, Mussolini was doubling his 100,000 troops already in East Africa. John was more interested to read that Amelia Earhart had set another record, flying 2,100 miles non-stop from Mexico City to Newark, New Jersey. Another article stated that the U.S. Navy had begun the greatest mass ocean flight ever attempted: forty-six planes were flying from Honolulu,

Pearl Harbor to Midway Island, a distance of 1,323 miles. One article said that the Royal Air Force was seeking recruits to keep pace with Germany's growing challenge, while another reported Russia was building an air arm and paratroop corps. Admiral Richard Byrd, home from a two-year Antarctica expedition, was meeting with President Roosevelt. John turned to the newspaper's entertainment page, noticing that the leading American movies playing at the London cinemas were "Devil Dog of the Air" starring James Cagney and Pat O'Brien and "Bride of Frankenstein" with Boris Karloff. At last the young pilot began to feel sleepy. As he glanced one final time at the front page his eye caught a small article, near the bottom, which stated, "Capt. Anthony Eden, Britain's traveling salesman of peace, returned from his Continental tour bearing a report of Benito Mussolini's avowed intention to wage war against Ethiopia." John turned out the light. Lying in the dark on his back, his arms folded behind his head, he wished for sleep as the sounds of this strange port city drifted through the open window.

# Train From Djibouti

In the morning a welcoming party arrived at his hotel led by the English-speaking host of the previous night. He was, John learned, a second cousin to the emperor. Dressed in white trousers and puttees, a dark cape, and a wide-brimmed felt hat, he introduced the other members of the party to John. Only one of them spoke English. They all boarded the French-owned woodburning, narrow-gauge train for the 488-mile trip to Addis Ababa along the only rail line in Ethiopia. John put away his burden of thoughts from the night before, turning his attention to the excitement of the exotic primitive land that lay before him.

The temperature along the Red Sea coastal plain was nearly 100 degrees Fahrenheit. as the train began its slow journey toward the cool fertile highlands of the plateau country. John had studied what he could find on Ethiopia, trying to familiarize himself with the geography over which he would be flying.

The country is referred to as the Tibet of Africa. Two-thirds of its territory is composed of highlands with elevations running from 3,000 to 10,000 feet and mountains ranging up to 14,000 feet. The highlands, the source of the Blue Nile, have fertile flatlands with cool temperatures due to the elevation even though Ethiopia is near the Equator. The plateau is slashed by plunging valleys and walled in by mountains. Where the land is level, strange shaped "Ambas", like the "buttes" of the American West, rear up in flat-topped pinnacles. The Great Rift Valley slices through the plateau, finally opening to the lowland desert and the Red Sea.

To the southeast is the harsh land bordering Somaliland, to the southwest humid tropical lowland. It is not the friendliest geography a pilot could wish for.

As the train pulled its slow, exhausting way up toward Addis Ababa, the capital in the highlands, John was awed by the beauty of this rugged country and shocked by the backwardness of its people and by the almost total lack of all things common to the modern Western world. The sunbaked mud huts and the camel caravans he saw could have been the same as a thousand years before.

His escort must have sensed his thoughts for he began to discuss the recent history of his country. "You of course know, Mr. Robinson, that Ethiopia is the only African nation that has been under exclusively black rule for at least three thousand years. It has been a Christian nation since 400 A.D. and because of that and the natural boundaries of mountains, deserts, and swamps, we have been isolated from the modern world for the most part."

"His Majesty is trying to awaken our ancient land, but as you can see, the bridge to the modern world spans a vast distance and must be crossed slowly. There were no written laws or penal codes of government in our country until His Majesty implemented the present constitution. Justice was dealt with by the rases or chieftains of each district. The rases are still powerful, and many look upon reform as a threat to their power, as do many leaders of the Coptic Church."

"The emperor has outlined administrative reforms and has enlisted the aid of such experts as de Halpert of Britain, Auberson of Switzerland, General Virgin of Sweden, and Everett Colson of your own country but changes must come slowly. The emperor does not wish to overwhelm his people. I am afraid you will see slavery in practice while you are here, but His Majesty has worked many years to stamp out its existence. The Italians use these sad facts against us in their propaganda. Nevertheless, a practice so long rooted in custom is not easy to abolish, as the history of your nation clearly shows. He has set up a bureau to administer the repression of slavery but still the Italians use it against us before the League of Nations."

John accepted a cup of tea and several plain cookies from a silver tray offered by a servant dressed in white. The train swayed and jerked on the narrow gauge rails. It slowed almost to a mule's pace as it began the gradual climb toward the highland plateau. They had passed the border of French Somaliland and were in low hilly country. On the rocky hillsides John could see an occasional round hut made of stones covered with a pointed thatched roof and surrounded by the weird cacti of the Ethiopian semidesert. He took a sip of tea and said, "What of your military situation? I have heard that some feel the emperor may have placed too much faith in the League of Nations."

His escort was very quick to point out that it was not his place or desire to comment on the judgment of the emperor. He then smiled, "But it is my task to inform you of the situation here, and I will be candid. We had hoped to receive some aid from England or France in the event the League of Nations could not prevent war, but we now realize we will receive very little aid if any. What is worse, an arms embargo has been declared against both Italy and ourselves which must make Italy happy. They manufacture arms, tanks and aircraft. We have only agricultural products and must import all manufactured goods, including, of course, arms. We have an army of maybe 300,000 men. Only a quarter of them have had any form of modern military training. Some of our young officers have been trained in England or France or were trained here by a Belgian military advisory group led by Colonel Leopold Ruel. Most of our armies will be led by their chieftains, the rases loyal to the emperor."

"We have 400,000 rifles of various types, very few machine guns, about thirty light and heavy antiaircraft guns, Oerlikons, Schneiders and Vickers. Most of our 200 or so artillery pieces are antiquated. We have a small, mixed batch of Ford and Fiat armored cars. The Imperial Guard is well-trained and equipped, but it is not large and is used to protect the emperor."

John had known before he left home that the situation in Ethiopia would not be promising if war actually occurred but he was stunned by the facts being given him.

"I just read that there are 200,000 well-armed Italian troops already on the border with more on the way. They are backed by 200 trucks, tanks and 200 aircraft. What can you do to hold against such odds?"

"You Americans are certainly straightforward in your questions." Then the ras smiled. "But why not, you have come a long way to offer your help. Your question and my answer must remain between us. If there is war, it will come from the Italians and the world will know it. The emperor has withdrawn his troops from the border to avoid any further incidents that could be used by the Italians as an excuse to attack. If they do, we will withdraw further to lengthen their supply lines. We have few roads, their mules will be of more use than their trucks over much of our land. Our best advantage is in our rough terrain and our soldiers. We have not been beaten in two thousand years by any outsider. Our soldiers need little; they are tough and zealous in their honor. In battle you will find them desperately courageous. They are fanatical fighters, they will stand or die for their homeland. But to win against the modern tactics of planes and tanks? Who has faced them? Could France or England, or Poland win against them? Who knows?"

He paused, then continued, "If war comes, the emperor will try to delay the enemy's advance and appeal to the leaders of the world to stop the fighting. If they will not, or cannot, we will fight for our land as long as we can."

John sat silent for a long moment. Then he said, "I've come a long way. Can you tell me where I will be needed and what I will be asked to do?"

"We badly lack means of communication. We have only a few radios, our telegraph service is poor and we have few roads. We will have to rely on our ancient method of using runners and drums. We have only a few aircraft at present, none of which is suitable for combat. None is even armed. Your job will be to use the aircraft for message delivery, observation, and any special assignment the emperor may need. The aircraft will often be our only rapid means of communications. In this country a plane can cross in two hours' time a distance it would take a man weeks or even months to travel.

His Majesty is anxious to meet you. You have come highly recommended. As you know, he was very disappointed in the flying ability of another North American brother of yours, Hubert Julian. Julian has returned to Addis Ababa."

John looked surprised. With a smile, the ras waved his hand. "He is assigned to training the infantry and will not be flying I'm afraid. The emperor is not in a position to turn down volunteers, but he did make the decision not to use Julian as a pilot. You yourself will be offered the rank of captain to begin with, along with the authority you need to conduct your air operations. We have, of course, some trained Ethiopian pilots now, and a few French aviators, but it is the emperor's hope that your experience will be put to good use."

John remembered the words of the pilot from the Great War he had met aboard ship. The man had said that when he volunteered for air service duty in France no one was able to talk him out of it at the time. With a knot

forming low in the pit of his stomach, John now knew
what he meant, and wished he had listened himself.
Ethiopia's plight was far more serious than his worst
fears. Then he thought, "Well, I've been afraid before,
but I've never been a captain," and he laughed out loud,
startling the somber group around him.

The train made frequent stops for fuel. It was a wood
burner, and the stops were a welcome break from the
long hours of sitting in the rocking, soot-soiled coach.
The drab, brownish vegetation began to give way to the
green of the highlands as the small engine pulled them
slowly toward the plateau country and the capital of
Addis Ababa. From time to time they would pass a small
band of warriors clothed in white shamas and waving
rifles, spears and swords at them. Some had lionskin
shields. "Lord, Almighty," thought John, "the Arabian
Nights caught in some kind of nightmare against modern
steel." He watched the sunset and thought of home as
the train chugged into the darkness, its hissing and
puffing echoing off the hills and canyon walls.

# Addis Ababa, 1935

Addis Ababa stood like an outcropping from the parched Abyssinian plain. The rainy season, which runs from June until September, had not yet had time to wash the city or turn its surrounding farmland green. Unlike the rural homes he'd seen—circular houses made of stone, clay, or woven bamboo with thatched cone-shaped roofs—the houses of the city were mostly one-room huts of sunbaked mud and wattle, or plaster-covered wood structures with corrugated iron roofs in various shades of rust. A few were two-story houses with outside staircases leading up to rooftop verandas.

Near the center of the city were some Western style houses, apartments, and hotels. Accommodations were waiting for Robinson at the Hotel de France. John felt he had entered a strange fairy tale world, or had passed through a time barrier into the days of the Arabian Nights. Caravans of camels and donkeys carrying everything from spices and foods to carpets, tins of fuel, or firewood moved through the streets. The marketplace was filled with the contrasting costumes of the different tribes and peoples of the country. There were Gallas and Danakils, Somalis, and Tigres, Cottus and the Hamites or "black Jews" from north of Lake Tana. The people spoke in Amharic, the official language, and in Tigrinya, Gallinya, and ancient Ge'ez.

Women wore brilliantly colored garments. Some had veiled faces. Others had gems in their noses or wore amber necklaces or gold earrings. John noticed a slim tan-skinned woman who wore a flowing white shamas. She flashed a quick glance at him with beautiful almond eyes, and disappeared behind a black-robed man who rode slowly along on a donkey in the shade of a huge umbrella carried by a servant who trotted alongside the beast. John was in the capital of the "Hidden Empire" and it was beyond his wildest imagination.

His hotel was located in a district which assumed a more modern, and Western semblance. The presence of other foreigners was evidenced by the flags of various countries who had diplomatic representatives in the capital. Upon his arrival at the hotel he was shown to comfortable quarters, assigned two servants, and told that there would be a small dinner gathering that evening where he would meet some of the people with whom he would be working. He was also told that he would be free to rest and tour the city for a few days, for the emperor could not receive him until the following Tuesday.

It was Friday and John welcomed the chance to have a few days to look around on his own. He bathed the soot and dust of the journey away, made his two servants understand that he was a week behind in his laundry, put on the only clean trousers and shirt he had left, and went down to the hotel bar where he was immediately met by members of the foreign press corps. It embarrassed him to learn that in the States news writers were referring to him as the "Brown Condor" of Ethiopia.

After a session of questions which John found difficult to answer since he had only just arrived, and after denying that he'd had anything at all to do with the emperor's decision not to let Julian, the "Black Eagle", fly for Ethiopia, he pleaded thirst and excused himself from further questions.

He had been astonished by the last question. He turned to Jim Mills of the Associated Press and asked, "Where did they dig up a question like that? I don't admire the guy, but I have never even met the emperor, much less influenced his decision about Julian." He took a slow sip from his glass and added, "Though after I found he was over here, I was relieved to find he would not be flying. He's done enough to damage the efforts of Negro aviation."

"Well," replied Mills, "You have to admit it would make a good story: a private war between two colored pilots from North America who had volunteered their aid to Ethiopia."

"From what I've seen, the Italians are going to give you writers all the stories you need. Why brew trouble for me before I even get unpacked?"

Jim Mills was about to protest innocence when in walked Hubert Fauntleroy Julian, who had, as it turned out, just been asked the same question by a reporter on the hotel steps. The "Black Eagle," now an infantry instructor, was more than a little upset.

The newsmen had evidently told Julian that Negro papers back home were claiming that Robinson had been the one to convince the emperor that Julian should never again be allowed to fly for Ethiopia. He burst into the lobby and, upon seeing Robinson, asked him angrily who concocted such a story and accused Robinson of trying to steal his style.

Underneath John's quiet and serious demeanor there was also a short fuse, and before Mills could get out of his chair to step between the "Condor" and the "Eagle" there suddenly were war bird feathers all over the hotel lobby.

It took the entire press corps to separate the two and force them to retreat to their respective rooms. Before they even had time to repair the minor damage to themselves, the palace sent word to them and to the press corps that there would be no more such displays. With the Italians on the border, the emperor wanted no personal feuds between his two North American blacks.

They both could draw aid and volunteers from the United States, and were therefore too valuable to be allowed the spoiled sport of petty scandal. His Majesty let it be known there would be no more fighting between the two of them.

After a bath and change of clothes, John showed only minor signs of the fight except for a large bump on the back of his head. A short time later there was a knock at the door and a messenger informed him that it was time to leave for dinner.

The Citroen sedan slowly made its way across the capital then went through a gate in the old wall, settling down to a twenty-five mile an hour pace on a rough road leading toward the countryside. The night air was chilly and the breeze through the open window felt pleasant to the three passengers crowded into the back seat. They had left beind the only paved road in the country; it had been paved for the Negus's coronation.

The word Negus, meaning leader, had long been used to refer to the emperor of Ethiopia, and John found himself wondering if news of his scuffle with Julian would find its way into the papers at home. Images of headlines referring to the Negus's niggers fighting on Saturday night caused him to curse at himself for allowing the stupid incident to happen. He had come halfway round the world, volunteered to risk his life in order to gain favorable publicity for blacks, and had begun by displeasing the emperor and giving the press exactly the wrong kind of publicity to send home.

At least tonight's dinner would be a very small, informal affair where he could perhaps unwind and relax a little. His companions in the sedan were Mulu Asha, an Ethiopian pilot recently trained in England, and Charles Chaudière, a French airman and mechanic who had been in the Emperor's service for some time. Both spoke English. In fact, most of the men in the air service spoke either English or French.

It was to be a traditional evening at the home of a wealthy friend and supporter of the palace. As the driver pulled the sedan to a stop, John was surprised to see that the home of Ras Tamru was a round mud-and-wattle walled thatched-roofed structure called a *tukul*. This one was larger than others he had seen, its walls white-washed. Any resemblance to the similarly shaped homes of the poor he had seen ended with this outward appearance. The strong wooden door opened to reveal an interior of huge proportions. A stone and copper fireplace was in the center and thick draperies formed small partitioned areas within the round structure. The floors were covered with large, thickly woven rugs. Two lionskins were spread near the fire which served as the center of activity, being used for both heating and cooking. Around the area were Western-style furnishings. To one side was a group of chairs arranged around a small table. Except for the fire, the only light in the room was provided by oil lamps. At the top of the cone-shaped roof there was a round opening which served as a natural chimney.

John was introduced to his host, though not to his interpreter who throughout the evening would stand in the shadow of the chieftain and step forward whenever his services were needed. After a round of polite talk about John's trip, the American concern over the threat of war, and inquiries as to whether or not John had found his quarters satisfactory, the host motioned for the group to take seats around the small table. When all had settled in their chairs, one of the two women who had been busy preparing food over the fire gave each guest a cup filled with *talla*, a native beer brewed from barley. The conversation changed to a discussion of flying in the region and of what kind of weather to expect. The men told a few light stories that seemed to put everyone at ease. One thing was clear. These people seemed to know a great deal about John's qualifications and flying experience and certainly a lot more about his home country than he knew about theirs.

Mulu Asha explained to John that the huge pancake-like loaf which was placed on the small table was the staple bread dish of Ethiopia. It covered the entire top of the table. Mulu explained that it was made from teff and cereal grain and was called *injera.* He also added that he hoped John liked it because he would very likely end up eating a lot of it if war came and he found himself away from the capital and its few restaurants.

From a pot, a spicy sauce with small chunks of meat was ladled right onto the *injera.* John turned to Charles Chaudière and asked how they would eat it. He had been given no plate and no fork. Chaudière shrugged and with a smile and a heavy French accent said something about, "When in Rome," then realizing he'd mentioned the capital of the Italian enemy, laughed and corrected himself, "I mean, of course, Addis Ababa." John then turned to Mulu who said something in Amharic to the host whereupon the host laughed, turning to John and motioning for him to watch. With his fingers he tore off a bit of the *injera,* folded it slightly to keep the *wat* (sauce) from running off, and put it into his mouth, following it with a sip of *talla.* John nodded, tore off a small piece, and managed to get most of it in his mouth, spilling only a little down the front of his suit.

He was surprised to find that not only did he have to eat *injera* with his own fingers, but from the fingers of others, since it seemed to be part of the Ethiopian's custom of hospitality to feed their guests. There was more than one course of *wat.* When John got up courage to ask what might be in the fiery mouthfuls that seemed to be flying into his mouth from all directions, Mulu and

Chaudière took turns checking off the list—lamb, goat, beef, chicken, eggs, ox tongue, cheese, peppers and spice and anything else that might be handy. Surprisingly, he found it tasted pretty good, but he wondered whether or not the concoction would blow his insides apart. When he mentioned this fear to his companions, and the interpreter passed his comments along to Ras Tamru, their host laughed and called to a servant to bring fresh cups filled with a golden orange liquid called *tej*. Mulu explained that *tej* is a wine made from fermented mead and honey, and that if a cup or two failed to quench the fire of the belly, several cups would certainly take one's mind off the problem. After a few sips John wasn't sure it wouldn't just take one's mind, period.

The ability to understand one another's language appeared to grow in direct proportion to the flow of the native amber wine. Amharic, English, and French were all exchanged as if everyone present understood perfectly what each person was saying, the *tej* not only making everyone multilingual, but apparently placing the entire group in agreement with whatever was being said at the moment.

Thus, it is little wonder that when someone suggested that the group go back into town to further acquaint their new fellow pilot with the cultural aspects of Ethiopia, all present voted in favor. All seven loaded into the sedan besides the waiting driver and ventured forth.

The rainy season was beginning, and the cool air helped make the crowded back seat of the sedan a little more comfortable. It also helped to steady John's stomach, which he was sure had been on fire shortly after the meal had ended. Wherever he was being escorted, John decided that he would conduct himself in a manner that befit his new rank, if he still had any after the run-in he had had with Julian at the hotel.

As they entered the city he realized just how great a task Haile Selassie had set for himself in his ongoing attempt to modernize the nation. John could see that the sanitary problems of the capital city were enormous since there was no sewerage or waste disposal system. Trash was simply tossed into the streets. But John was not aware of the waste disposal nature had provided. As the lights of the sedan traced a path of light before them as they turned suddenly around the corners of the streets within the city, time and again the lights would illuminate the surprised face of spotted hyenas feeding on the evening's garbage. Had he been a drinking man, the sight of wild hyenas in the street might have been enough to make him swear off *tej* for good. None of his companions paid the least attention to the spotted beasts so John decided his one "God Almighty, what the hell are those!" was enough comment on the matter.

The sedan pulled up in front of a fairly modern structure with a large archway spanning two heavy doors, one of which was open. Inside, crowded around small tables, were groups of jovial Ethiopian men, eating, smoking, or sipping cups of *talla* or *tej*. There were a few Ethiopian women too.

John noticed several white faces scattered through the room, dimly lit by table candles and oil lamps. He assumed correctly that they were the *ferenghi* or foreign military advisors, members of the Western press, or perhaps some of the medical team volunteers he had heard about. He seated himself on a cushion on the floor just as a group of musicians struck up a wild rhythmic tune. He was served a cup of wine, which he was determined to sip slowly, and heard a voice behind him call his name.

He turned to see Jim Mills, the correspondent whom he had met at the hotel bar, sitting at the next table. "You are not doing badly for a new boy on the block."

Before John could answer a burst of applause rose from the crowd as several tall slim brown-skinned girls entered the cleared area in the center of the room and began to dance for the delighted customers. They were lovely to look upon as they moved to the exotic music. John turned to Mills and, glad for the company of a fellow American, remarked, "This beats hyenas for entertainment."

Mills laughed, "Speaking of entertainment, would you like a little company now and then during your stay?" He added, just before John could answer, "Of course, you might have to marry one."

"In that case no thank you." Robinson replied.

"Oh, it's not all bad. Which type of marriage do you want?"

John questioned, "Just how many types they got here?"

Mills explained, "Under Ethiopian custom there are three types. The first, foremost, and least common is the church marriage or *Qurban*. Now that one you have to be careful of. It is considered sacred and indissoluble. Young people are considered too unstable for this type of marriage. The second type, called *semanya* is more common. It is a civil contract marriage blessed by a priest. It can be dissolved by mutual consent or court decision."

"And the third type?" questioned John, a little more interested.

"The third type," replied Mills, "is called *damoz*, or wage marriage. Traditionally, this kind of marriage is provided a man traveling far from home. You certainly qualify there. Its purpose is to provide such a man with a temporary wife. At the end of the marriage, no obligations are owed unless a child has been born."

"You know, that's the most intelligent approach to marriage I've ever heard. Mussolini says he is coming over here to civilize the savages of Abyssinia. He might do better to send the Pope over here to study marriage making."

Mills replied, "Oh but that won't sell as many newspapers as the idea of the seat of the Western Christian world making war on the oldest Christian nation in Africa! Hell, they even held Fascist Sunday, or some such nonsense to convince all those young conscripted Italian soldiers that God is on Mussolini's side. I'll tell you, Johnny, that bastard Mussolini and all his 'glory of Rome' rot means to have a war with these Ethiopians."

Jim took a long look around the room. "These bright, funny, proud, hospitable friends of mine just can't move this ancient nation into the twentieth century. Anyway, here's a toast, my Brown Condor, to you and me and all the other poor bastards who trade home for the wild winds of fortune." Jim Mills raised his glass, smiled, and said, "Happy flying."

# Rocks in the Clouds

The three engines of the Junkers trimotor droned with the strange harmonic tones caused by the slight variation in each engine's speed. The trio constantly moved in and out of synchronization. All the seats had been removed from the rear cabin, which was now filled with drums of aviation fuel to be off-loaded and stored on arrival in Adowa, near the Italian Eritrea border.

It was at Adowa in 1896 that the Ethiopians had soundly defeated an invading Italian army. Now, thirty-nine years later, the Italians were again massing on the Eritrean border in preparation for a new invasion. Il Duce, in promising his people a new "Roman Empire," had vowed to avenge the disastrous loss. Mussolini had been thirteen when word of the defeat had reached Italy. The news accounts had described barbarous atrocities committed by the Ethiopians and told of the death of 10,000 Italian men and the loss of seventy-two cannons.

The figures concerning the cannons had stuck in John's mind. Shortly after hearing the story, he had learned that almost half of the present pieces of the Ethiopian artillery were the same seventy-two cannons they had captured from the Italians in 1896! After looking over the Ethiopian inventory of aircraft, he was convinced they'd captured half their aircraft in the same battle. He had counted twelve old French Potez planes. They were small planes powered by Hispano-Suiza engines, only slightly improved over World War I aircraft. There was one Tri-Junkers, three Fokker trimotor transports and a huge old single-engined Farman. Not one of the planes was armed.

John looked down at the jagged terrain below from the Tri-Junkers he was flying. They had followed the road leading from Addis Ababa past Dessie where they had left its guiding ribbon. Then they turned slightly to the left across the beginning trickle of the Takkase River toward the town of Sakota.

From there another road led them to Adowa, now only a small village on the hot desert lowlands. Chaudière sat in the copilot's seat on John's right. The flight served three purposes: transporting a stockpile of fuel to Adowa; giving John a check-out of the Junkers transport, the largest and newest plane in the emperor's service; and familiarizing John with the landmarks he must memorize. There were few maps of Ethiopia and none were useful for flying. No radios or other modern navigational aids were available. A compass, a watch, and a good memory for landmarks and terrain features were the only means of navigation a pilot had in Ethiopia in 1935.

As important recognizable features appeared below, Chaudière would shout them out over the engine noise rattling the cockpit. He pointed out that it was extremely important to learn every valley, riff, river bed, road, village, and distinguishable rock outcropping, and especially to recognize the entrances of the valleys, canyons, and riffs. A pilot might fly up an unfamiliar canyon only to find that it narrowed too much to allow a turnaround, and that the ridges rose faster than the plane could climb. If such a canyon terminated in a dead end, so would the plane and pilot.

The central plateau plains were at elevations between 4,000 and 10,000 feet, and the highlands had peaks above 14,000 feet. There were almost always clouds in the high country and with the monsoon blowing moist air up from the ocean during the rainy season, the clouds and rain had been heavy during most of the flight. Mountain tops were playing hide-and-seek in the clouds. John realized that these clouds of Ethiopia had rocks in them. Had Charles Chaudière not known every trail, ridge, and rock along the way, and every compass course from landmark to landmark, John realized that they would have, early in the flight, made their mark in life at about the 10,000-foot level on the side of some ridge. Now, however, the terrain was dropping down to the coastal plain and the rain and clouds grew less frequent. John recalled some of the methods the mail pilots at home had developed to help them find their way along their routes in all kinds of weather. They would draw out their own maps, sketching important features along their route. Some of the notes might read "large barn with twin oaks at south end and windmill at east side by pond," or "river fork points north with two sets of rapids. Course 320 degrees from fork." If a pilot dropped out of a cloud or rain shower, or were flying above a broken layer of clouds, his life might depend on his ability to recognize with no more than a brief glance some feature on the ground that would tell him from memory his present position. John entered both in his notebook and his memory everything Chaudière pointed out to him. Ethiopia was about the size of Texas and Oklahoma combined. He had a great deal to learn.

There was no airfield at Adowa, just flat rocky ground on the edge of the town. It served well enough. The Junkers, like the Ford trimotor, was built of corrugated metal and was strong as a bridge. Its thick wing was capable of lifting an enormous load. The Junkers was a low wing design as opposed to the Ford's high wing. Both incorporated extremely tough landing gear with large wheels which allowed them to operate from rough unimproved fields.

The trimotor made one low pass over the village to alert the work detail of its arrival. John circled the field to look it over and lined up for the landing. He spread his right hand over the three throttles and eased them back, keeping a little power on to gentle the heavily loaded plane onto the ground. The clattering flat sides of the metal Junkers and the banging struts of the landing gear announced contact with Mother Earth as the plane waddled over the rough field, raising a cloud of dust in spite of the recent rain.

When John shut down the engines he could only hear the ringing in his ears. He realized how tiring the long flight had been for him. It always took a little while for his transition from sky to ground, but he slumped in his seat longer than usual before reaching to unfasten his safety belt.

"Not bad," he heard Chaudière saying. "Not as good as Chaudière, but none the less, not bad," said the Frenchman already out of his seat.

"We'll be here for the night. By the time they get out here, unload and refuel us, it will be too late to return to the capital before dark. Clouds, and rain, and the mountains are bad enough, even for Chaudière, but clouds, rain, mountains, and darkness with no lighted cities below us, that is impossible!"

Making their way past the cargo to the door, they stepped out into the heat of Adowa. It was quite a change from the cold drafts which had filled the cockpit at 12,000 feet a short time ago. Both men were quick to pull off their flying jackets as they ducked under the wing to sit in the shade until the work crew had gathered.

"We'll stay long enough to oversee the refueling of our old girl here. Never trust anyone. Check the fuel from every barrel that goes into your tanks. I found one barrel from which someone had stolen half the petrol and replaced it with either water or camel piss, both are about the same color around here. On another occasion a drum had leaked most of its contents which had pooled in a depression in the dirt. The poor bastard who was in charge was so afraid he would be accused of stealing that he scooped up the stuff with a pan and put it back in the drum. Petrol is precious as hell over here, but not when it's full of sand. I think you get the point of the story."

John shook his head. "This is getting to be more fun all the time." He looked at Chaudière and asked, "How long have you managed to stay alive at this game?"

"Four-and-a-half years, but if the war comes, it will be all your game. My government would frown on a Frenchman fighting the Italians."

"Oh, that's just great!" John said in a quiet, deliberate tone. He climbed up on the wing and took a funnel with a built-in filter from Chaudière as the fueling crew arrived. The Frenchman joined him as the crew began to pass up the fuel in tin containers which they filled from the large drums.

"Don't look so left out." Chaudière said, "After all, this war is between you Ethiopians and the Duce."

"Hell, you know I'm not Ethiopian. My country doesn't want me to fight the Italians either."

"You will be," Chaudière smiled.

"Will be what?" asked John.

"Will be an Ethiopian, my friend."

"Now tell me just how you figure that."

"It is simple. When the emperor receives you, he will already have my report on your excellent ability and qualifications. He will honor you by bestowing upon you rank, salary, and Ethiopian citizenship. Surely you will not refuse such an offer from the emperor himself."

"Did he offer you citizenship?"

"I am afraid the color of my skin prevented him from making such an offer, but he has been most generous in the area of pay. It would be ungrateful of me to complain. C'est la guerre."

"You crazy bastard, you won't leave if the Italians start a war."

"No, but we won't tell France I am fighting the Italians, and we won't tell America that you are an Ethiopian. We crazy bastards must stick together, eh?"

# Witness to War

The rain had stopped for a while and the sun broke through the clouds to brighten the morning. For John, it was a good omen. He walked past the recently doubled guard detail at the gates of the Imperial Palace. Regulars in the Imperial Guard, the only well-equipped unit in Ethiopia, wore the greenish khaki uniforms of the Belgian army. Their caps had been made in Japan. In contrast, most of those called to arms wore traditional white shamas and went barefooted. Their white garments would make fine targets, John thought.

From the gate he was escorted by a sword-carrying guard dressed in white and wearing puttees but no shoes. John followed him past two lions chained beside the walk leading up to the palace steps. One lion watched their progress with his deep staring eyes and yawned nonchalantly as they passed. The other lion was asleep. They reached the steps of the weathered but well-structured palace, built by King Menelik in the late nineteenth century. Greeted by a chamberlain of the emperor's staff, John was led into the palace.

He hoped the excitement he felt would not show as two massive, carved doors swung open and he walked into the vast office of the emperor of Ethiopia. Before him was a magnificent carved desk. To the side and behind the desk stood a cavernous marble fireplace. To the left, sitting on a plush Oriental carpet was a chair of gilt and red brocade, bearing the imperial crown and insignia. The chair was occupied. John bowed as he had been instructed by the chamberlain.

The face of the small bearded man who sat in the gold chair appeared weary, but his bright eyes shone with warmth and dignity. John returned the smile, and grasped the handshake offered him by His Imperial Majesty Haile Selassie I, emperor of Ethiopia, King of Kings, Elect of God and Conquering Lion of Judah.

The emperor motioned with his hand and the royal interpreter was summoned to his side. After the chamberlain withdrew, the emperor spoke in Amharic to John Robinson.

"His Majesty bids you be seated," explained the interpreter. The conversation was held person to person through him since the emperor preferred to speak his national language although he often answered before the interpreter had time to translate the visitor's English into Amharic. The emperor understood several languages including English and French, perfectly.

"Welcome, John Robinson. We are honored and deeply grateful that you have traveled so far to offer your services to Ethiopia."

John replied that it was he who was honored to serve His Majesty, a man he had long admired. "I hope my ability as a pilot will be of some use to Ethiopia."

"My staff and I have studied your qualifications, and the reports of your performance by our own air group since your arrival. Excellent reports. I would like you to consider the following offer. As you must know, we are in the process of training Ethiopian pilots, but none have yet attained your skill, and especially your experience. We have therefore continued to rely on our French airmen to lead our air service. If war cannot be avoided—and I pray it will be—but if it cannot, the French staff will be placed in an awkward position. France insists that these men cannot fight against her neighbor Italy. Belgium, likewise, is anxious to avoid giving offense to Italy, and the official Belgian military mission here will be withdrawn in the event of war. We have arranged for certain Belgian volunteers, some from the Congo, to return as advisors, however, they will not be able to enter actual combat and risk embarrassment to their native Belgium.

"The same is true for our French flyers. As in the case of the Belgian advisors, they cannot be discovered on the front lines. Flying they could risk capture, and because of the color of their skin, they certainly could not pass for Ethiopians. Also, under stress of war my people will have some natural suspicions I'm afraid, of the *ferenghi* white advisors. Therefore, the offer I make to you is this: the rank of colonel and the command of the Ethiopian Air Corps, along with Ethiopian citizenship. As an American, your nation will not allow you to hold rank or fight in the army of another nation. Of course, on the other hand, publicity of your activities in your home press will, I selfishly admit, gain popular support in America. You will, of course, be properly rewarded for your services. But, please take your time. I realize that in asking you to accept my offer, I am presenting you with a most serious decision. We respect your need for careful consideration."

John took a long walk and thought over what he had seen and learned over the past few weeks. He thought of home and the relative security of the flying school he had established, now run by his long-time friend Cornelius Coffey, and the promise of a future flying school at Tuskegee. But it was the summer of 1935 and the world was changing, he knew.

In July of 1935 Senator Clark, a Democrat from Missouri, had called for a full investigation of all lobbying on Capitol Hill, particularly that done by large utility companies. News items noted that Japan was at war with China. Wiley Post was making the final test flights for a new float plane he planned to fly with Will Rogers from

Los Angeles to Moscow via Alaska. In Mississippi, the Key Brothers, Al and Fred, had set a record endurance flight in a modified Curtiss Robin monoplane using in-flight fueling. The flight had lasted twenty-seven days, five hours and twenty-four minutes.

Walking down a rain-soaked street halfway round the world, another flyer who had grown up in Mississippi, John Robinson, was now a colonel in the Imperial Air Corps of Ethiopia. He carried in his breast pocket two passports, one American, the other Ethiopian. He wondered if he would ever be allowed to use the former again. An 1818 U.S. law forbade American citizens to accept commissions in a foreign army at war against a nation with whom the United States was at peace. His smart uniform, in cut, resembling that of the RAF, brought admiring glances from the women he passed in the marketplace. It also made him more than a little self-conscious. In a letter to his mother, he tried to explain his situation. He was a black man in the only continuously black-ruled country in Africa but he knew little of its language or customs. He was a colonel. He was often in the company of an emperor who, through his appeals for peace before the League of Nations, was becoming a focal point of world concern. He was making more money than he had ever made before. The air corps was small and its equipment dated, but he was to be given its command. He wondered if anyone at home really cared. He did not tell his mother, but he knew from world news and from talk at the palace that Ethiopia was being thrust into harm's way.

The following Sunday, the emperor Haile Selassie attended church services carrying a rifle to dramatize the fact that, though Ethiopia was praying for peace, she was willing to fight if necessary.

Ten thousand miles away a picture of the emperor at church with a gun was carefully cut out of an American newspaper and placed with John's letter in a small drawer of a bedside table. There was a Bible on the table. Celest Cobb sat on the edge of her bed and closed the drawer. "Lawd," she said, "Please be with my boy Johnny."

Two political cartoons appeared on the pages of American newspapers. One showed Mussolini juggling arms and treaties while a bystander told Hitler and Stalin, "It might pay you boys to watch this guy a little longer." The second cartoon pictured Hitler giving Mussolini a medal for breaking up world peace machinery and the ring of nations around Germany. To appease Italy, France and England had secretly agreed to keep out of "the Abyssinian thing." The League of Nations could argue but not act to keep peace.

For one last time Haile Selassie, with tears in his eyes, rose to plead for peace for his country before the League of Nations. As he began to speak, Baron Aloisi of Italy walked out of the League of Nations and the Italian consuls were withdrawn from Ethiopia.

It was September of 1935, and Cornelius Van Enger, U.S. chargé d'affaires in Addis Ababa advised all U.S. citizens to leave Ethiopia.

On the 28th of September the following message was issued by means of telegraph, donkey, runner and drums:

> All men and boys old enough to carry a spear will be mobilized and sent to Addis Ababa. Married men will take their wives to carry food and cook. Men without wives will take any woman without a husband. Women with small children need not go. Those who are blind, cannot walk, or for any reason cannot carry a spear are exempted. Any able man who is found at home after receipt of this order will be hanged. Signed: H.I.M. Haile Selassie I.

The day before, General de Bono at his headquarters in Asmara, the Eritrean capital, had received the following peremptory telegram from Il Duce: "Order you to attack at dawn on third, repeat, third October."

Just before dawn on the third of October the young Italian troops assembled on the bank of the shallow Mareb river. They sat, finishing breakfast, checking equipment, or talking in small groups. Young and a long way from home, they recalled the stories of how in 1896 the Ethiopians had castrated Italian prisoners, which made them more than a little nervous about being a part of Mussolini's "New Glorious Rome."

Each man had been issued four day's rations, a half gallon of water, and 110 rounds of ammunition. As the sun rose de Bono's three columns crossed the Mareb on a forty-mile front. The Italian army was composed of a hundred thousand men with an equal number held in reserve, backed by 6,000 machine guns, 700 pieces of artillery, 150 tanks, 140 aircraft, several thousand motorized vehicles and 6,000 mules. It was the beginning of a Fascist march that would end peace and engulf the world in a decade of war.

Ten thousand feet above and slightly to the south of the front a tiny speck in the sky went unnoticed by the columns marching below. Their banners flew and their trumpets blared in the triumphant style befitting the new conquerors from Rome. The speck was an obsolete French Potez plane, its engine throttled back to reduce noise. Its lone pilot, a young black man from Gulfport, Mississippi, looked down on the invading army and unwittingly was the first American to witness the prologue to the Second World War.

He was too busy to think of the historical significance of what was unfolding below. Having taken off before first light to routinely observe the border, he found himself gathering data on an ongoing invasion while keeping an eye out for Italian aircraft—the single engine Imams or tri-engined Marchettis or tri-engined Caproni 133's that could easily outrun his old Hispano-Suiza powered Potez.

He turned southward pointing the nose slightly down to gain speed as he descended toward Adowa. He shivered and wondered if it was from the chill of high altitude or cold fear. "Well," he thought, "it was fun for awhile." And it had been during the preceding weeks —the training, the meetings, the parade in Addis Ababa where Belu Abaka, the nearly seven-foot tall drum major of the Imperial Army Band, had led the procession past the emperor's magnificent pavillion specially erected for the occasion in Cathedral Square. John had stood with the emperor on that occasion. The crowd temporarily forgot its war-fever when the emperor's royal lions escaped from their cages. The crowds of people had scattered and the lions had to be caught or shot before the people would return so the ceremony could continue. "But now, my God." John exclaimed to himself, "It's happening. War, Jesus!"

Like many of the Italian boys below, he wondered, "How was it allowed to happen? What the hell am I doing in the middle of it?"

On the second day of the invasion the Italians were still marching into Ethiopia. No shots had yet been fired. The emperor had decided to abide by the conditions imposed on him by the League of Nations which had fixed a twenty-mile-deep neutral zone along the border. He also decided not to engage the enemy until they were well inside Ethiopia and dependent on long supply lines. He ordered the establishment of battle lines forty to fifty miles from the frontier. This meant the abandonment of Adowa without resistance. John was ordered to remain in Adowa as long as possible in order to report the latest information about the Italian advance. He planned to leave on the sixth.

On the fourth of October, Ras Seyonm Mangasha withdrew his small force that had made brief contact with the oncoming Italian forces, and took shelter in a cave at Maryam Shoaitu. On the following day, from his mountain hideout he saw a large number of trimotored aircraft approaching Adowa from the direction of Eritrea. As they reached the town, he saw large balls of flame and smoke erupt in puffs below the planes. Moments later the distant rumblings of exploding bombs reached the Ethiopian chieftain.

In the center of Adowa, the first explosion had awakened John. The second nearly blew him off his cot. Half-dressed, he grabbed his shoes and ran into the street just as a Caproni trimotor flew overhead. At the same moment a group of Ethiopian warriors entered the street from a building that had been hit. They appeared bewildered. Angry and frustrated, they drew their swords and shook them at the attacking aircraft. The citizens of Adowa and the soldiers were terrified. None of them had ever witnessed the sights or sounds of artillery, much less bombing. The only aircraft many had seen was the little Potez which John had taken the precaution to hide on the outskirts of the town. Now the sky was full of aircraft of the Regia Aeronautica. They had broken formation and were bombing at random.

John had never seen anything like it. Though he had tried to prepare himself, the shock of war still stunned him. The roaring planes overhead, the explosions, the screaming and yelling all around him added to his sense of helplessness. Deciding that his place was with his aircraft, he began to make his way toward the edge of the town where he hoped he would find the Potez still hidden and safe.

The streets were full of men, women, and children running in all directions through clouds of smoke and dust. Hundreds were wounded or dying. Several explosions occurred nearby. John stumbled and fell upon what he discovered to his horror was only half of what had been a human being. John's uniform became caked with a crust of blood and dust. He lifted a crying, blood-splattered baby from the body of its dead mother and handed the child to a woman sitting dazed in a nearby doorway. The bombing had stopped by the time he reached his plane. As soon as the last of the Italian aircraft had departed for Eritrea, John took off for Addis Ababa to deliver news of the bombing to the emperor.

The next day, the sixth of October, the Italians marched with great fanfare into Adowa which had not fired a shot in resistance. In Rome there was joyous news that at last the Italians had been "avenged" by their new victory, while in Adowa, after the trumpets and speeches of the victory celebration had died down, some of the Italian troops found themselves wondering if a dusty, poor, insignificant village like Adowa could really be worth a war. The most powerful war machine Africa had ever seen halted while General de Bono consolidated his forces and brought up supplies for the next advancement deeper into Ethiopia.

In Addis Ababa Haile Selassie listened gravely as John related the details of the Italian advance and the bombing of Adowa. When he finished John added, "I must tell you also that there are rumors that some of your generals and troops will desert or go over to the Italian side. I have heard this both here in the capital and while I was in Adowa."

The emperor did not change his expression. "This is true. Italian agents have been in the country for a long time, and I am afraid some of my people are in their pay. But we will fight without them when the time is right."

Then he smiled and said, "But you, John Robinson, have served me well. It will now be your duty to serve as my personal pilot. You will be based here. You and your pilots will carry my dispatches to the front."

John bowed, and walked toward the door.

"Colonel Robinson," the emperor asked, "I know you have asked for a faster plane. There is an embargo against us that prevents me from obtaining a military plane. Is there perhaps a civilian plane that might do?"

John replied, "Your Majesty, there is a small American firm, Beachcraft, that is making a fast new cabin plane. I believe it would make a good courier plane."

# Dogs and Rabbits

When John reached his suite he felt empty, tired, and lonely. He was surprised to find his rooms spotlessly clean. There was a bowl of fresh fruit on the table by the couch. He was even more surprised when the door to his bath opened and he found himself staring at a slim brown young woman with beautiful eyes who returned his gaze with a shy smile. She wore a white kamis, a long loose dress with a gold chain around the waist.

"Please," she said and held out her hand.

"Who are you?" John managed to say.

"Please," she repeated, as she was often to do. It was the only word of English she knew. She stepped forward and took John's hand and led him beside the bath which was filled with hot steaming water. Before he could decide what he should do, he found himself naked, sitting in a hot tub, with the girl kneeling beside him massaging his tired body and gently bathing him. He was too tired to be embarrassed, and too in need of company that evening to ask any questions. Whenever she said please, he simply did as she motioned for him to do. When she had finished drying him after the bath she led him to the bed. There she smiled and gently kissed his lips. John wanted to cry, to laugh, to hold her desperately close to him, wanted not to be alone.

She moved softly next to him and he held to her tightly. They did not speak.

She held him until he fell asleep. Then she gathered up his dusty soiled uniform, laid out a fresh one on the chair next to his bed, and let herself out of the apartment.

The following morning while he was having breakfast with Mulu Asha, John mentioned the girl who had been in his room.

"I'm afraid I had something to do with that, but what happened was not planned," Mulu replied.

"You mean you know what happened?"

"Yes, she came to me early this morning and told me. She is no concubine, my friend. She is the daughter of a chieftain, a ras, and the former wife of a friend of mine who was a fellow student pilot. He was killed in a training accident at flying school in France. She has admired you from a distance since you first arrived."

He continued, "Yesterday, after I brought you from the airfield to report to the emperor and dropped you off at the palace, I saw her near the square and told her the news from Adowa. When she asked about you, I described how upset you appeared. She asked if she could do something, perhaps prepare your rooms, see that all was in order. We knew you would need rest. She took some servants and saw that your suite was cleaned. You had left it in a mess nearly two weeks ago. She said she dismissed her servants and intended to leave after drawing your bath. That is when you returned and found her there. You are better known by our people here than you realize, my friend, somewhat of a hero. Anyway, when she saw how tired and shaken you were, I think she lost her head and perhaps her heart for the moment. Great God, you don't know how shocking you looked to us. You were covered with caked blood and dirt. There was the usual oil on your face, your uniform was torn, you looked dreadfully older."

"Please, what is her name, will I see her again?" asked John.

"My friend, I think it is best that you not know who she is for now. She is a little afraid to see you. And there is her family to consider. This is no ordinary lady, my friend. We will have to wait and see. Besides, my commander, you and I are going to be busy it appears."

"I want a name for her," said John. "What is the Ethiopian word for 'lady'?"

"Waizero," replied Mulu.

"All right, tell her I don't have to know who she is. I will call her 'Waizero', but I want to see her, to be with her when there is time. We don't have to be seen by anybody. I won't embarrass her. Will you tell her that for me? Maybe the three of us could meet together."

And so they did, often the three meeting to dine or picnic in out-of-the-way places, sometimes at the farm of their friend Ras Tamru. There were quiet times when John and his "Waizero" were alone. He learned some words of Amharic and she learned a little English, but she did not reveal her true identity and John never asked. He knew he needed her.

In the months that followed she was beauty and peace when most of the world was filled with ugliness, frustration and the horror of war.

But that morning there were other things to think about. John and Mulu were joined after breakfast by the French pilot Chaudière.

"What I saw yesterday is gonna happen a lot more and there is nothing we can do as far as trying to help the army stop it," John told them, "except by keeping them informed of where the Italians are and carrying orders and messages. The idea of putting guns on the planes we fly makes about as much sense as putting spiked collars on rabbits. Put either of them in a dog fight and they'll lose their hides. I want every pilot to understand that if he sees or thinks he sees another aircraft, he can bet it's an enemy, and he has orders to run like hell and save his plane, not to mention himself."

"Mulu, you will be in charge of covering the southern border with Italian Somaliland. The emperor is certain that the Italians will open a second front there. Charlie, while there is still time, you will use the trimotors to transport as much fuel as you can to our front line and enroute landing strips. It won't be enough but it might save some of us until the pack animals can deliver more. After that we must keep one trimotor safely hidden. It's the only thing we have to transport the emperor if he insists on flying. You will also have to continue to take charge of maintenance. We're probably going to need parts from two aircraft to keep one of them flying. We have twelve flyable planes and twenty-five pilots, and most of them have less than a hundred hours. That means a handful of us will do most of the flying. I meant what I said about the Italian planes. Even they are growing old-fashioned compared to what is being designed today, but they can catch anything we have, and they have 200 to our twelve."

The three climbed into their "staff" car, a 1930 Fiat, and headed for the airfield. The field was fairly new. The first few years of air operations had taken place on the race track and polo grounds. The foreign diplomatic set, however, had been so irate at this interference with their Sunday sport that the emperor finally gave in to their complaints and ordered an airfield constructed on the outskirts of the capital.

As the car moved through the streets Chaudière started to sing an English translation of a bawdy French song popular during the first World War, only he changed the words to inflict terribly funny insults on the Italians. Johnny and Mulu loudly joined in the choral refrain. Chaudière remembered at least twelve verses and after that the men made up new lyrics and new insults as they went along. Then, slowly the laughter died away.

They sat in silence until Mulu said, "I'm the only one that has to be here. You both volunteered and therefore you are both crazy."

"No, my friend," said Chaudière, "it is the world that has gone mad. We laugh because, as men, we are afraid to cry." The car stopped in front of the hangar at the field because there the pilots and ground crews had assembled for instructions. John smiled because all of the Ethiopian ground crews and half the pilots had refused to wear shoes.

"O.K.," said John, "let's get started."

General de Bono was conscious of the vast numbers of Ethiopians available for war, the only advantage the Ethiopians had against the modern Italian army. He chose to halt the Italian war machine after the towns of Adowa, Adigrat, and Makale were secured. He intended to consolidate his position before launching his next advance. He stressed caution in his communications with Il Duce.

Mussolini was of a completely different mind, however, and the messages from Rome impatiently requested the immediate resumption of the Italian advance. The advance on Makale, directed by orders from Mussolini, had left the flank of the Italian army uncovered. When yet another order from Rome demanded that de Bono resume the march without delay, the general balked, indicating in his reply that Il Duce's tactics were defective. Six days later de Bono was informed that he was being replaced by General Badoglio.

Badoglio arrived on the twentieth of November only to recognize, as had de Bono, that a consolidation before the next stage of campaign was indeed essential. It was not until the twentieth of January, in fact, that Badoglio was willing to resume the initiative.

It was a difference in character, not strategy between the two men that was to greatly alter the nature of the war. De Bono was basically a gentleman warrior. He saw his role more as a pacifier of the Ethiopian people than as a conqueror. He had no trouble establishing peaceful

relations with the populations in the towns that had
fallen.

Badoglio had a different outlook. His single aim was
to engage the Ethiopian army in open battle and destroy
it by any means. De Bono had refused to employ what
were referred to as "special" weapons. Unfortunately for
the Ethiopians, Badoglio had no qualms about using any
weapon he possessed, even if it was illegal according to
the international codes of warfare.

As winter advanced, so did an Ethiopian counteroffen-
sive. Because of rival jealousies, Italian bribes, and dan-
gers of internal revolts, Haile Selassie chose his generals
for their loyalty. None of them had military expertise or
even military training in the normally accepted sense. A
few young officers had graduated from St. Cyr, the
French military school. Yet in late 1935, Ras Seyoum
Mangasha's force of 30,000, Ras Kassa's 40,000 men, the
30,000 man-force of Ras Mulugeta (a seventy year old
warrior who had in his day suppressed a number of
revolutions), and Ras Imru with another 40,000 men
began to force the Italians back from the Takkaze River.
In a two-month period, they drove them back to Axum
and to the Warieu Pass, threatening to drive Badoglio's
troops out of Makale.

John continued to carry reports between the capital
and the front. One concerned a battle between Ras
Imru's forces and a group of Italian and Eritrean troops
armed with twelve of the CV 3/35 two-man Italian "Flea"
tanks armed with twin 8mm machine guns.

The Ethiopians, some carrying spears, first attacked
the Italian force and then cut off its escape route. The
Italians moved their tanks up to smash through the
Ethiopian formations drawn up on the crest of the
mountains at Amba Asar. As the tanks began to rumble
forward and approach the Ethiopians, the emperor's
troops broke formation, not in retreat, but in attack. In

John C. Robinson (Courtesy National Air and Space Museum)

Class in Aeronautical Training at the Curtiss-Wright Flying School, 1931. (Left to right) Jack Snyder, Bill Jackson, unknown, unknown, John Robinson (suit), Amber Porter, Janet Waterford (Bragg), Joe Mulgrow, Cornelius Coffey, Harold Hurd. (Courtesy Harold Hurd)

A 1929 fund raising dance to benefit "The Afro-American Youth in Aviation." The airplane pictured is a Heath Parasol built by John Robinson and Cornelius Coffey. Robinson is in the extreme left, Coffey is kneeling in the middle. (Courtesy Cornelius Coffey)

Robbins Airport (All Colored), managed by John C. Robinson, 1933. This was the headquarters of the Challenger Aero Club. (Left to right) George Mitchell, Albert Cosby, Clyde Hampton, George Webster, unknown, Janet Waterford, Doris Murphy, William Jackson, Harold Hurd, Dale White, John Robinson. (Courtesy National Air and Space Museum)

Janet Waterford Bragg. (Courtesy Harold Hurd)

OX5 International Airplane. (Left to right) John Robinson, Joe Muldrow, Dale White. (Courtesy Harold Hurd)

A.J. Neely, of Tuskegee Institute, bids "good luck" to John C. Robinson as Robinson prepares to take-off from Tuskeegee for return to Chicago in 1934. (Courtesy National Air and Space Museum)

"The Brown Condor" in Ethiopia. (Courtesy Harold Hurd)

Colonel John C. Robinson receives a hero's welcome as he returns to Chicago from Ethiopia. (Courtesy Harold Hurd)

# TWENTY THOUSAND HAIL ROBINSON

Picture taken from the balcony of the Grand Hotel, where Colonel John
C. Robinson made his first public speech after arriving from Ethiopia.
(Courtesy Harold Hurd)

Colonel John C. Robinson (Courtesy Tuskegee University)

Barnstorming in Florence, Alabama in 1936. Cornelius Coffey and an unknown passenger stand beside the 4-place Curtiss Robin airplane marked "John Robinson Airlines." (Courtesy Cornelius Coffey)

the face of deadly crossfire from the tanks, the Ethiopians, running en masse, engulfed the steel machines by sheer weight of human flesh, preventing the Italian crews from further using their machine guns. The Ethiopian soldiers literally tore the tracks from the vehicles. By sundown, the Italian force had lost almost half its troops.

For the Ethiopians it had been a victory, a small victory, but an important one for Ethiopian morale. They had pushed the Italians back for the first time. They had also exposed the Italian flank and Ras Imru now began to hammer away at it as Rasses Seyoum and Kassa engaged in a siege against the Italians at Warieu Pass.

At the same time Ras Mulugeta pushed against the Italian Third Corps so the Ethiopians could encircle the town of Makale and recapture it. By January twenty-second, General Badoglio drew up a plan in the event of a retreat from Makale. If he were forced to withdraw, it would mean moving 70,000 men, 14,000 animals, and some 300 guns down a single road.

The Ethiopians had pushed the Italians back even though they had never before been subjected to air attacks. They learned to move by night and attack by dawn. The Italians laid down murderous artillery fire and were supported by tanks. Still, the Ethiopians blazed away with their rifles, attacking and infiltrating the Italian front, in many areas engaging in hand-to-hand battle, as wave after wave of Ethiopian soldiers surged forward to assault the Italian fortifications.

Badoglio ordered the use of a "special" weapon. From the sky fell a "terrible rain that burned and killed." It was *yperite*—mustard gas sprayed from the skies and from artillery shells and bombs. The Ethiopians could not understand it. They were terrified, yet they still tried to fight. By the twenty-fourth of January the battle of Tembien Province was over. The Ethiopian warriors could not stand up to the fierce firepower and to the deadly clouds of mustard gas that blistered their skin and lungs, and blinded their eyes.

The Italians had closed another phase of the war, but Tembien left them uneasy. The Ethiopians had fought against impossible odds and had pushed the Italians back, inflicting more than twelve hundred casualties.

John Robinson had seen the terrible price the Ethiopians had paid in the battle of Tembien. From the air, some areas of the battlefield looked spotted with patches of snow. The patches were piles of warriors lying dead in their white garments. The Ethiopians had lost more than eight thousand men. Those warriors who had been able to retreat were pounded by the planes of the Regia Aeronautica.

Mussolini's sons, Vittorio and Bruno, and son-in-law, Count Ciano, all flew Capronis and took part in many of the indiscriminate bombing raids conducted by the Italians. Vittorio would later record his experiences in "Flight Over the Ambas", recounting the brutal activities of the Regia Aeronautica. He described the bombing of the Ethiopians as fun, making white flowers appear—the flowers formed by the white-clad bodies of Ethiopian troops being blown into the air by the exploding bombs.

John had flown far forward, leading two larger planes carrying medical supplies to a front-line aid station run by an Egyptian Red Cross unit. One of the supply planes was flown by Count Carl von Rosen of Sweden. It was the count's own plane which he had fitted out as a flying ambulance.

There were many such volunteers. Count Hilaire de Berrier offered himself as a pilot. (He would later be captured by the Italians.) There was an impressive list of volunteer doctors from all over the world in the Ethiopian Red Cross: Dr. Robert Hockman of America; Dr. George Dassios of Greece; Dr. Shuppler of Austria;

Dr. Hooper of America; and Dr. Balau of Poland. The British Ambulance service was commanded by John Melly who would later die in the service of the emperor. Field hospital and medical teams were sent by Sweden, Finland, Greece, Norway and America.

As John looked down on the scattered dead he thought to himself, "Jesus, fifty volunteer doctors, for an army of half a million men who have to go on taking this kind of beating."

John had violated his own rule by flying so close to the Italian lines. He had thought there would be little Italian air activity now that the battle of Tembien was finished and the Ethiopians had melted away in retreat. He was wrong. From the corner of his eye he caught movement. Far to the north he saw two specks growing larger.

John, though an experienced pilot, had no combat training. His plane was unarmed, and he had never been shot at. "Come on, rabbit," he said to himself, "Those dogs are after my hide" and he pushed the throttle forward to the stop. The two planes coming slowly up behind John were Imam bi-planes. They were 700-horsepower, enclosed-cockpit, fighter-reconnaissance planes and there was no question they would outrun his old Potez.

As the miles passed beneath him, John knew his only hope was to trade the sure danger of being shot down for the risk of flying into the cloudsl that lafy hovering over and among the tops of the low mountains ahead. There was no reason for him to maneuver until the Italians got within firing range. It would only serve to give up more of what little distance remained between the Potez and the Imams. A slow straight line to the clouds was faster than a slow curved line. He had to reach the clouds.

Three miles separated him from the snowy clouds when he looked back and saw orange flashes coming from both the Italian machines. They were firing at him! He began to use his rudder to skid his plane from right to left as he continued on for the clouds. Both Italians were so anxious to be the first to shoot down an Ethiopian plane that they flew abreast of each other and were interferring with each other's shooting.

With a mile or less to go before reaching the clouds, John suddenly felt a popping vibration as bullets tore into the tail section and left wing of his plane. He thought of the trick his instructor, Johannsen, had used one playful afternoon in Chicago when they were returning from a lesson. A fellow instructor in a faster plane had gotten on their tail and, in spite of his aerobatic skill, Johannsen had been unable to shake him off. John hoped the old Potez would hold together, especially after being hit, while he tried Johannsen's stunt. Quickly he checked to be sure the Italians were closing in on him. Indeed they were as more of their bullets slammed into his right wing. Suddenly he yanked the throttle all the way back to idle. He pushed down full left rudder as he pulled back hard on the control stick. The Potez whipped into a snap roll. The world spun violently as John's plane snap-rolled to the left. At the same moment, the glass gauges on his instrument panel shattered and he felt a hot burning just above his left wrist. The plane pitched up as the snap began bringing the cockpit into the line of fire of the Imams just behind and to the left of John's plane. The Imams shot past the Potez's wing as they veered sharply to keep from ramming it. Upon over-shooting the Potez, both Italians immediately racked over into steep turns to the right thinking that they now had become targets. When they realized that the Ethiopian was not turning to fire on them but was running straight, they continued the circle until they were once again coming into firing position behind it.

John knew the mountain stream several thousand feet below him ran down a narrow valley. He lined up with the stream and plunged into the cloud.

The Italians were not willing to be so foolish. They turned and chased up and down the wall of the cloud believing no pilot in his right mind would long stay on course in those clouds. They expected him to circle back out, and they would be waiting for him. Besides, if he stayed in the clouds, well, the Italians concluded the clouds would take care of him. These clouds had rocks in them, which the Italians could see since the tops of the mountains stuck up through the cloud layers.

Inside the cool but bumpy white fluff, the sweat rolled off John's face and hands. He could feel the hard knot of near-panic swelling up in his throat. His mouth was dry. When he entered the cloud, he was careful to stay in a slight climb holding steady airspeed. He had to keep a compass course lined up with the mountain stream that he knew ran up the valley—if it was the right stream and valley.

He concentrated on keeping the compass needle still, the airspeed exactly the same. If the compass tried to move, he was quick to use the lightest amount of rudder to stop it. He knew that he could not hold the plane steady for long in the cloud. His plane was not equipped with gyro instruments. His compass and airspeed were the only instruments he had left.

He had escaped the Italians. But unless he broke out of the clouds he would lose, either to vertigo or to a mountain or, more than likely, to both.

The grey of the cloud began to lighten, then to grow bright. Suddenly he broke out of the cloud into clear sky. He was startled to find that he had been in a shallow turn. Directly in front of him was the rocky slope of a mountain ridge! He banked sharply away from the ridge, brushing another cloud. He continued turning and twisting to avoid both cloud and rock until he was set at last on a course that would lead him home.

The clouds below were broken and became scattered as he flew southward so he could see the land features below. He realized that he was shaking all over, especially his knees and ankles. His face and arms felt numb with extreme cold. He was short of breath.

He had not seen the Italians since he entered the cloud. He knew he must be over 14,000 feet, maybe higher. He could not tell—his altimeter was smashed. He began a descent as familiar landmarks started to appear below.

As he descended to lower altitudes, the numbness of the cold began to wear off. It was then that he became aware of a stabbing pain in his lower left arm. He could not move his left hand from the throttle. He looked down to see why. His lower sleeve was dark red. The fingers of his flying glove were stuck to the control with clotted blood.

By the time he landed an hour later, there was a throbbing pain over his whole left arm. An 8mm bullet had passed through the flesh of his arm. It had chipped the bone, but not broken it.

As his arm was being dressed at an aid station, John mumbled to himself, and the doctor made out the word "rabbit." "What's that you said about a rabbit?"

John replied, "I said it's gonna be hard to go back and tell my men about a dumb rabbit that nearly got caught by the dogs."

# For the Glory of Rome

**B**y late October of 1935 Haile Selassie realized that the faith he had placed in the League of Nations had been a mistake. Not one of the great Christian nations of the world would act to bring an end to the invasion of his country and to the slaughter of his people.

Though the governing bodies of the world would not act, there were demonstrations of support for the Ethiopians by people in many countries. In England three thousand young men volunteered to fight for Haile Selassie. In America demonstrations such as a rally of ten thousand blacks and whites in Madison Square Garden and a black boycott of Italian-owned stores in Birmingham were held throughout the country. In Cairo the faithful prayed to Allah to spare Ethiopia. Even in Fascist Berlin a film entitled *Ethiopia 1935* carried an anti-Italian theme. Statesmen all over the world expressed their grave concern as though they intuitively realized that the invasion of Ethiopia foreshadowed universal conflict, yet they could not organize effective ways to put a stop to Mussolini's aggression.

Emperor Selassie not only had seen his hope of aid from the League of Nations fade but he had also witnessed the defection of several of his chiefs, including one of his own sons-in-law. Accepting Italian bribes, they took as much as ten percent of the emperor's troops with them over to the Italian side.

Haile Selassie acknowledged that his loyal followers had but two choices: either submit to becoming an Italian colony after three thousand years of self-rule, or continue to resist Fascist aggression alone, with no hope of aid.

The battle of Tembien had shown what a terrible price in loss of lives he would have to pay but his council of chiefs, supported by the fierce pride of his people, left him only one choice—to lead his people as long as they had the will to defend their land.

The emperor was not blind to what lay ahead for his nation. To boost his soldiers' morale he determined that he should be seen among them. This decision placed a heavy responsibility upon John Robinson—that of safeguarding the life of the emperor of Ethiopia.

American newspapers carried a small feature, among the many articles concerning the Italo-Ethiopian conflict, stating, "Piloted by John C. Robinson, a Negro from Chicago, Emperor Haile Selassie made his first plane flight in several years in order to inspect Ethiopian defenses." It was the first of many flights the emperor would take, making his life dependent on the flying skills of the black airman from Mississippi.

Mulu Asha continued to transport messages and supplies to the southern front, returning with reports of Italian activity there. During the early stages of the conflict, the Italians had established a line running from the Kenyan border to British Somaliland, paralleling the border of Italian Somaliland. The Italian forces along that line had been given the role of establishing a purely defensive secondary front, a role that did not please one ambitious Italian commander. His name was General Rudolfo Graziani, a man who had claimed, "Il Duce shall have Ethiopia, with or without the Ethiopians."

Badoglio on the northern front had been given ten divisions while Graziani, for his defensive role, had only one Italian division. He set out to change that role by spending his time opening new roads and expanding port facilities. He also motorized his division by buying hundreds of motor vehicles supplied mainly by American manufacturers via British car dealers in Mombasa and Dar es Salaam. He communicated his desire for action to Mussolini, who proved more than willing to listen.

At first Mulu brought promising reports from the southern front. The two Ethiopian armies of the south were commanded by very different leaders than those of the north. One was Ras Desta Damtu, another of the emperor's sons-in-law, the other was Ras Nasibu who had traveled extensively abroad. Both were young, loyal and progressive. With the aid of an old but knowledgeable Turkish officer named Mehmed Pasha—better known as Wahib Pasha—who had come to the aid of Ethiopia because he loathed Mussolini, the troops of the southern armies were better trained and equipped than those of the north.

In the early battles the Ethiopians on the southern front had held against Italian probes, knocking out many of the light tanks upon which the Italians depended for supporting fire. When the tanks became bogged down in soft terrain, the Ethiopians crept up to them and fired into the weapon slits in the armor. But the Ethiopians could not attack directly. Even when they tried to march only at night, they were spotted by Graziani's reconnaissance planes and subjected to incessant bombing by the Regia Aeronautica.

Mulu brought back reports of the Ethiopians' faltering under the Italians' constant air attacks. He also told of the effects marching through the harsh desert with poor rations, malaria, and dysentery had on the troops. However, he was able to report that deep behind the southern front the fortifications of the cities of Harar and Ogadon and a defense line, all organized by Wahib Pasha, were manned by Ras Nasibu's army of 30,000.

In early January 1936, John, Chaudière, and Mulu Asha were all three in Addis Ababa. They had managed to gather together the makings of a small feast at a time when rations were becoming lean even in the capital which now was subject to bombing raids. A lamb was prepared for dinner and drink was supplied by their French companion who produced a store of choice wine from his seemingly endless supply.

The three sat on cushions, talking at first not of war but of the times they had spent together before the fighting began. They ate, drank and reminisced about the beauty of the Ethiopian landscape which they had introduced to John during his early flying routes over Ethiopia.

"Yes, it's a mighty pretty country, different from what I had imagined it would be," John remarked. "To tell the truth, Mulu, I thought it would be all desert and camels. Some of it is raw and primitive, but I've also seen the green valleys, and the mountains, and the rivers like the Omo cutting and carving its way into Kenya. It's beautiful. I wish my folks at home, especially Momma, could fly with me to Lake Tana and follow the beginnings of the Blue Nile and see the rainbows in the waterfalls and watch the sun light up the clouds that rest on the mountain tops."

"I believe, my friend," replied Chaudière, "that you have the romantic soul of a Frenchman."

"I believe only that you both have been deep into French wine," smiled Mulu, "but I am pleased by what you say, especially after considering the situation that has brought you here. It is not very pretty, and we all know that it can only get worse. The emperor knows it, too. There is only courage and sadness left in his eyes. But my friends, let's drink Chaudière's wine. Which reminds me—Chaudière, I hope you have your supply hidden where the Italians won't find it."

"Hell," said John, "if you and I haven't found it with me sending him off on flights just so we can look for it, I know damn well no Italian's going to find it."

"So that is what you two do when Charles Chaudière is in the air!" The Frenchman refilled all glasses and continued.

"You are untrustworthy friends and terrible flyers, but this is war. What can one expect? So I will share my source of supply even though you are undeserving: I get the wine from a friend at the field hospital here. The good doctor has two cases brought in each month marked 'medical supplies'."

"Oh, hell."

"What is the matter, John?"

"You didn't hear? The hospital was bombed today. Dr. John Melly was killed; nurses were wounded; the damned Italians are hitting all the medical units. They seem to aim at the big red crosses marked on the field hospitals. They blew up Count Rosen's ambulance plane last week at Quoram. He told me they have repeatedly tried to hit it. I know damn well they can see the red crosses painted on his wings."

"I thought tonight we would not speak of such things. Here and now for the moment, our bellies are full, the wine is from another and better year, and we are together. Let's drink to that."

It was the last time the three would ever be together. The next day Chaudière began supervising the uncrating and assembly of a new American plane, a Beechcraft, whose parts had just arrived by train, while John flew Haile Selassie to Dessye. Mulu Asha flew south to the border army led by Ras Desta.

On the southern border near Kenya where the Ganale Doria river crosses into Italian Somaliland, General Graziani had assembled supplies and had strengthened his Italian division by bringing up several divisions of Eritrean Askaris. At dawn on the twelfth of January, Graziani opened a battle that would become known as the massacre of Ganale Doria by dropping nearly two tons of mustard gas on the Ethiopian positions.

Mulu Asha was awakened by the bombardment. He reported to the message center and was ordered to deliver dispatches to Addis Ababa. His plane, covered with brush, was hidden off the tiny cleared landing strip. He just managed to get it uncovered when the first wave of Marchetti SM 81 trimotored bombers roared overhead. Their wings had been painted with large orange sunburst paint schemes like that later used by airshow stunt pilots. The special paint was designed to make the craft easier to find in search attempts should one go down in semi-desert regions. Shells exploded around the small Ethiopian aircraft. Mulu and his crew rushed for cover. A bomb exploded just in front of them. Mulu did not remember hearing the blast. When he awoke the cool air of dawn had been replaced by midmorning heat. Sounds of fighting surrounded him: rifle fire, explosions, screams, shouting.

Something was wrong. Something was not working. He fought nausea. His mind cruelly regained consciousness. And then the pain. His left eye was not working. His face and his arms were on fire. His throat and lungs were raw, he could not take a full breath. He crawled over the body of one of his ground crew, then staggered to his feet. He saw that his plane was a smoldering wreck. He tore at his canteen and poured water down his burning throat. He poured it over his face and tried to wash the foul-smelling liquid from his arms.

"What's happening?" he asked hoarsely of a passing Ethiopian rifleman.

"Move, we have orders to move back, we can't hold." The rifleman looked at Mulu a moment, then turned and quickly moved away to join others in retreat. Mulu joined them, asking where he could find Ras Desta's headquarters. No one knew. Unable to find medical aid, he followed his retreating countrymen.

The Italians had outflanked the Ethiopian forces. Organized in mechanized columns, they were rounding up and shooting the dispersed remnants of Ras Desta's army, who fled on foot through camel thorn bush and across burning sand.

The few wells that lay along the path of retreat were captured by the Italians. On the second day, Mulu ran out of water as did all of the Ethiopians. Most had no food. The Ethiopians had to leave their badly wounded behind. Those who could walk did so as long as they could.

The Italian planes fired continually on the retreating Ethiopians. Mulu was splashed by mustard gas. His arms and face were masses of raw blisters. His blind left eye became infected. As he staggered on, though he did not realize it, he breathed in audible moans and cries. The pain kept him from resting at night.

On the fourth day he was part of a large group that had managed to reach the river of Ganale Doria. The cold blessed river. All Desta's men could think about was their crying need for water. Crazy with pain, Mulu began to run toward the river. He stumbled. Fighting for breath, he got up and began to run again. He could see the water, the longed-for river bank.

Suddenly there was machine gun fire from across the river. Cries rang out along the bank on his right and left, he heard shouting and shooting, but still he ran toward the river. The pain in his left eye was unbearable. His face was blistered beyond recognition. A new pain tore through him, sharp pain. He stumbled and fell. Pain! He was pain! He was screaming but he did not hear. He crawled, he could see the water. Sharp staggering, hard pain again. Mulu collapsed and still he moved toward the water. He pulled himself with his raw blistered hands down the bank and touched the water and lowered his face into the muddy, bloody river. After four days without water for one brief second he felt its coolness on his poor face.

Mula Asha was dead. They were all dead.

The Italians had reached the river first. Setting up their machine guns they had waited until the remnants of Desta's army, crazed with thirst, reached the river bank, then shot them down like hordes of stampeding animals.

The road to Neghelli, capital of the southern Galla Borana district, now lay open to General Graziani but just to make sure, he ordered forty tons of bombs dropped on the city. On the twentieth day of January he occupied Neghelli for the glory of Fascist Rome.

# Warriors and Sportsmen

John and Chaudière did not know the fate of their friend and fellow pilot. After news of the defeat of Desta's army reached them, their hopes that Mulu would turn up among the few survivors of the battle of Ganale Doria faded as the weeks passed. John had lost other friends but after the loss of his closest Ethiopian friend, he felt depressed and tired. He could not understand why a seemingly uncaring world did nothing to stop Mussolini.

Robinson continued flying his unarmed plane between Addis Ababa and the front lines across skies controlled by Italian fighter planes. These flights were the chief medium of communication between the emperor and his forces on the northern front. Somehow John continued to get through. Because of his success, Colonel Robinson was selected by the Italian fighter pilots as a prime target.

In a letter to his friend and former student, Harold Hurd, John told of flying conditions at the front.

> The only thing I can say for myself is that I am trying to do my best in what ever mission or duty I have . . . We are having a hard fight over here with our limited amount of modern war equipment, but every man, woman and child is doing their part to help and I am sure with God's help and our courage we will come out OK in the end. Sometimes I have to fly for two weeks without pulling my shoes off, and with very little sleep in between time; this is when I am along the Northern front, but I am only too glad that I am doing my part to help. These conditions might help to finish my flying career . . .

At home the press carried stories of the conflict, often mentioning the American flyer, John Robinson. Especially in Chicago which considered itself the home of the "Brown Condor." Considerable interest in John Robinson was also evident in New York.

He was becoming a hero in the States, particularly in the ANP (The Associated Negro Press). All the Aid to Ethiopia groups as well as all the African Methodist Episcopal Church groups raising funds to aid the Ethiopian cause considered John their representative there.

The Gulfport newspaper, *The Daily Herald*, carried articles about John. John's family was rightfully proud of him. Like all mothers, however, Celest Cobb could read between the lines of her son's letters. Sometimes when she was alone in her kitchen, she would hold in her small hands, a newly arrived letter, or a clipping from the paper, and feel the sadness that she knew must lie in her Johnny's heart. Too proud of him to show her tears, she would quickly dry them with her cotton apron and busy herself with some household duty.

In Ethiopia John busied himself with the task of test flying the newly acquired Beechcraft. Chaudière thought it the most beautiful plane he had ever seen. Many would agree with him even to this day. It was a cabin bi-plane with a negative stagger to the wings. The lower wing was farther forward than the upper, which reversed normal bi-plane design. It was clean of line and had another feature designed to increase speed: retractable landing gear. It also had gyro instruments, which meant it could be flown safely in clouds without needing outside references of horizon or ground features. It was officially called Beech-17 L but was nicknamed the "staggerwing." Having only a 225-hp Jacobs engine, the L model was less powerful than its prototypes, but Beechcraft had found it sold better in the money-tight years of 1934 and 1935 than the larger engined models.

Though it was also slower because of the smaller engine—the more powerful models could do 200 mph

—John was happy to find that his staggerwing would do an honest 175 mph. It was fast enough to keep the Italian planes from catching him. The staggerwing was also rugged and had a low landing speed that would allow him to use short landing areas. He would also no longer have to freeze to death at high altitudes. In the Beechcraft five people could fly in the comfort of a heated cabin. On the ground the staggerwing could be tricky, quick to reward a gear and wing-bending ground loop to a pilot who let his attention drift on landing, but in the air it would do anything a pilot asked of it.

John and Chaudière wasted no time in gaining experience flying it. They took turns learning to fly just by referring to the instruments. One would wear a hood fashioned from cardboard that prevented him from seeing anything but the instruments while the other would sit in the copilot's seat as a safety pilot and instructor. With practice they learned to climb, descend, turn, and hold a given course, all by reference only to the flight instruments.

The emperor took a special interest in the beautiful new plane and was pleased by John's praise of it. The "rabbit" had turned into a fox. The few times he could not outrun the Italian machines, he easily lost them in the almost everpresent clouds. His one fear was for the plane to be caught while on the ground. Though he suffered three mustard gas attacks (which affected his breathing for several years) on the ground, he did not give the Italians another chance to shoot up his plane.

To many members of the Regia Aeronautica, the Disperata and Quia Sum Leo squadrons, the war had turned into a sport. They were unopposed. Many Italian pilots came to view the strafing and bombing of "target of opportunity" as shooting practice.

There were some hazards, however. Two such "sportsmen" were engaged in shooting a patch of "savages in need of civilizing." They had discovered the group after dropping their bombs on another target and were taking turns strafing the terrified, hungry, and exhausted warriors, clad in their traditional white shamas. The warriors were not without courage. There was nowhere left for them to hide and they could run no more.

One of the young Italians taking his turn at the strafing run noticed that many of the Ethiopians had stopped moving and were now firing at him with rifles. He pulled up and started to turn for another run, looking down to watch his wingman as he made his strafing attack. He noticed that his friend curiously did not pull up in a turn but instead began a slow climb in the direction of the Italian lines. He made a last run and then flew in the direction of his friend, who was now flying low. The reason became obvious. A thin trail of smoke streamed back from his friend's left engine. The engine on the nose of the Caproni had stopped. A stream of white vapor trailed from the right wing. It was fuel pouring from the wing tanks. With only his right engine running, the pilot of the stricken plane could not hold altitude. He picked a rough but reasonably clear area in the valley ahead and put the Caproni down among the brush and scrub of the rock-strewn terrain. The second Caproni circled low overhead and happily rocked its wings when the pilot of the downed aircraft stepped from the cabin door and waved.

It was late in the day. Because Ethiopia is near the equator the sun sets rapidly. The pilot of the second plane knew it was already too late to effect a rescue before the next morning. He did not have enough daylight left to seek help. Flying low over the ground, he surveyed the landing path of the downed plane. It looked chancy at best. He pulled up and started a wide search pattern around the area, extending farther and farther out from the center.

About four miles away he saw what he had been looking for but hoped he would not find. He had not been the only one to see his friend go down. From a hilltop a group of about two hundred Ethiopian soldiers had also observed the smoking Italian machine go down. Spotting a band of about thirty Ethiopians making their way down from the hill toward the landing site, he pulled up and around in a tight turn coming back at the scouting party and firing his 7.7 mm machine guns. With no hope of a rescue party reaching his friend until the following day, the young Italian emptied his guns at the Ethiopian party, slowing its progress.

One of the ironic truths of war is that the young of all nations possess courage and pride. These are the very qualities that are used to bring about their slaughter.

The young flyer did attempt a rescue of his downed comrade. It was a gamble, but he felt compelled to make it. The sun would be down within thirty minutes. The Ethiopians were maybe an hour-and-a-half away from his friend. He throttled back as he lined up with the landing area the other Caproni had successfully used. Slowing his plane to just above stalling speed, he dragged onto the landing site with a little power so as to land at the slowest possible speed and shorten the landing roll. His wheels touched. The plane rolled and bounced along the rugged ground, the high wing just clearing the scrub brush, the props chopping through some of the bushes.

The plane slowed rapidly and the pilot began to relax just a little. He could see his friend running toward him. Then without warning the right wheel slammed down into a hole. Though the wheel came up the other side of the depression, the jolt had been more than the landing gear could absorb. The landing strut had cracked. As the plane continued to roll, the same wheel bounced over a rock the size of a shoe box. When the weight of the plane came back down on the cracked strut, it gave completely and the wheel sheared away. The plane swerved violently to the right as the wingtip slammed into the dirt. The right propeller churned up rock, dirt, and brush as the plane settled to an angle on its right side and slid to a stop. The pilot quickly shut down all the engines and evacuated the plane but there was no fire. Just silence, two lonely friends, and the setting African sun.

"Mother of God, you should have left me. You could have brought back help to find me in the morning."

"I'm afraid not, my friend. There are others who have already found you. Now they will find us both. They are coming from that hill over there. Do you have any suggestions?"

"We can't very well fight them off till morning. Yet, if we leave the planes we may not be spotted by search aircraft."

"If we leave the planes, we will have to make it all the way to our lines without being seen. I don't know. It must be thirty miles or more."

"It really doesn't matter." As he spoke the Italian drew his pistol and crouched beside the wreckage of the plane. "Your friends have arrived in record time."

A shot rang out from the brush, then a second, then a third and fourth. Ethiopian runners had been sent out ahead of the main party to find and pin down the Italian prey. They did their job well. Firing occasional shots from several surrounding areas they held the flyers at bay as the last rays of twilight gave way to darkness.

The two young flyers sat back to back, pistols drawn, waiting to be rushed from any or all sides.

"Save the last bullet for yourself. You know what they did to the last flyers they caught."

"Yes, you need not remind me." They both remembered the report a month earlier of the fate of two fellow Italian airmen downed at Daggah Bar. After their capture they had been ordered beheaded by an Ethiopian commander.

The Ethiopians were expert in the art of night infiltration and knife attacks. While the two Italians waited in the darkness to be rushed by attacking riflemen, the Ethiopians were drawing straws. The winners, four in all, were allowed the honor of making a knife attack.

"I am sorry to have caused you this trouble. You were crazy to try to pick me up, but I want you to know I am grateful to you, my friend."

"I too am sorry, but you would have done the same. Now we finish it together."

The next morning, not far from the two wrecked planes, a pair of hyenas cautiously approached. Overhead the vultures had begun to circle. The young Italians stared up at the sky with wide, glazed eyes. Their feet were bare. Their boots and jackets had been taken. Below their chins their throats gaped open from ear to ear and flies swarmed over pools of clotted blood. As the vultures flapped down to the ground nearby, they engaged in rude debate with the hyenas over how to divide the spoils of war.

Badoglio's army on the north cautiously pressed on toward the capital. One by one the Ethiopian armies were destroyed. Ras Mulugeta was killed at Amba Aradam. The armies of Ras Seyoum and Ras Kassa had been blown to pieces by the Regia Aeronautica which rotated its aircraft in such a way as to keep at least a dozen planes over the battlefield at all times during daylight hours. (It was a technique to be used by both the Allied and Axis powers during World War II.)

Only Ras Imru's forces remained stubbornly undefeated. Badoglio prepared to fight Imru by adding to his supplies 48,000 artillery shells, seven million rounds of small arms ammunition, and hundreds of tons of bombs. The Ethiopians had no more reserve arms available and often attacked surrounding Italian positions armed only with swords and clubs. Haile Selassie had reason to be proud of his troops.

On one occasion the Italians recorded the interrogation of a mortally wounded Ethiopian officer. When asked who he was, the man replied, "I am the commander of a thousand men." When asked why he did not lie down on the stretcher, he replied that he preferred to die on his feet. "We swore to the Negus that we would hold against you or die. We have not won but we have kept our promise." He pointed to the valley. It was littered with 8,000 dead. He joined them before nightfall.

To the south, General Graziani was having a more difficult time. He had run into the "Hindenburg Wall," the defense line that had been designed and set up by the old Turk, Wahib Pasha, who from his headquarters in Bulale, acted as advisor to Ras Nasibu.

As April 1936 arrived, the beginning of the rainy season added to Graziani's problems. The earth turned to mud and the rivers became difficult to cross. In one ten-day battle the Ethiopians dug in at the Jerar River. Firmly lodged in caves and hollows, they also dug trench positions among the roots of trees. Graziani employed another of his "special" weapons. To eliminate the Ethiopians entrenched in the caves, the Italians brought up flame throwers to within a few yards of the cave entrances. The flame throwers were supported by tanks. In fact, some of the small tanks were themselves converted to flame throwers—the fuel for the weapons was carried in special armored trailers pulled behind the tanks and connected to them by hoses. With bombs, artillery, tanks, flame throwers, poison gas, and motorized infantry, Graziani finally broke the "Hindenburg Wall."

John was called to fly the emperor once more. There was only one 40,000-man army left. The Negus himself would lead the last battle. Unlike so many of the foreign volunteers who had drifted away as the situation had grown steadily worse, John was determined to serve as long as he was needed. He was shocked to see how worn and weary the small dignified figure seated in the cabin behind him appeared.

The Imperial Guard forces had been sent ahead to await the emperor's arrival. In the plane the emperor's party sat in silence knowing the battle ahead would be the last large defensive effort. When they landed, Haile Selassie turned to John. "Colonel John Robinson, you have served me and my people faithfully and well. You have endangered yourself unselfishly. You have done all that has been asked of you. Go home now. There is little you can do here any longer. You must try to get out if you can. Try to tell your nation what you have seen. I have not been able to make the League of Nations understand. If they refuse to act in the future as they have refused to stop Fascist aggression in Ethiopia, then what you have seen here is not ending, it is only beginning."

John could say nothing. He bowed his head. "Take my hand, friend," the emperor extended his hand and John grasped it, with tears in his eyes.

"Thank you, John Robinson. I pray we meet again."

# Stranger to Peace

Across a lush green valley near Mai Ceu, 31,000 Ethiopians faced 40,000 Italians and Eritreans. Another 40,000 Italians, held in reserve, were distributed between the Belago and Alagi passes. Haile Selassie later sent a message to his wife about the battle, stating, "From five in the morning until seven in the evening our troops attacked the enemy's strong positions, fighting without pause. We also took part in the action, and by the grace of God remain unharmed. Our chiefs and trusted soldiers are dead and wounded."

With only 20,000 of his men left, the emperor ordered his troops to retreat. Because the few Red Cross hospitals had been bombed out of existence, the Ethiopians could do nothing for their wounded but carry them. The retreating soldiers were under constant air attack as they moved toward Lake Ashangi. Enemy planes dropped seventy tons of explosives on the exhausted Ethiopians. Then the planes returned to spray the area with mustard gas. Men and pack animals were blasted to pieces. The waters of Lake Ashangi became gas contaminated. Thirst-crazed troops who drank it died from poison. The emperor would later be quoted describing the scene: "It was no longer a war for the Italian airmen. It was a game . . . it was a massacre."

At the end of April, Haile Selassie conferred in Addis Ababa with Sir Sidney Barton, the British foreign minister, and Monsieur Bodard, the French ambassador. He informed them that his Imperial Council had decided he should not join Ras Imru, as he wished, to organize a guerilla war at the gorges of the Blue Nile. Haile Selassie

also told the foreign minister he did not have the means
to defend the capital. He and the Ethiopian government
would try to escape into exile in the hopes of returning
one day. The minister arranged for the treasury's gold
to be deposited in Barclay's Bank in Jerusalem. Barton
promised the emperor that if he could reach the port of
Djibouti in French Somaliland (the rail line was still
open), a British ship would transport his party to safety.
Because of the number of foreign citizens on board, such
as the diplomatic community and world press representatives, Mussolini refused to give his commanders per-
mission to bomb the train that carried Selassie to French
Somaliland. While the Italian people were rejoicing in
their great victory, Haile Selassie sailed from Djibouti
on May 4, 1936, aboard the British cruiser H.M.S.
*Enterprise.*

John arrived in France with little baggage and almost
no money. He felt relieved to be safely away from the
senseless slaughter in Ethiopia, but he felt apart from the
bustling scenes of people moving about in their normal
day-to-day routine, living in the ordinary fashion of the
Western world. He tried to enjoy his stay in Paris, but
he could not adjust to the people's apparent lack of
concern about what had been happening in Africa.

One evening, an old Frenchman who spoke English
said to him at dinner, "What can Ethiopia teach us about
war? I was in the Great War. I already know about such
things. It will never happen here again. We are building
the Maginot line."

Everyone seemed too busy to be concerned.

The French government did seem to be mildly
apprehensive about the new German claims to territory
controlled by France since the defeat of the German
empire after World War I. The newspapers claimed that
Hitler was moving troops, disguised as civil policemen,
into the Rhineland. In Spain civil war seemed certain.

Japan was engaged in aggression against China. An American general named MacArthur made a statement that he believed if another conflict should occur it would not be fought in trenches as the last one had been. Troops he said "would be highly mobilized, fighting mostly in the open, with fast units using tanks and trucks. Aircraft would play a great part in any conflict." When he learned of this remark, John thought to himself, "I could sure be a witness to the truth in that general's statement. But would anybody listen?"

John had escaped from Ethiopia and the Italians with little more than the clothes on his back. By the time he'd reached Paris he did not have enough money left to buy passage to America. He could not reach the Ethiopian government for aid or back pay due him because the emperor and what was left of his government were fleeing into exile.

John turned to his best friend, Cornelius Coffey writing him a letter asking if Coffey could send him enough money to get home.

It was 1936, the depth of the Depression and business, especially aviation business, was suffering. Coffey had bought a wrecked Great Lakes Trainer bi-plane and had painstakingly restored it to like-new condition. He had no cash reserves. Coffey sold his Great Lakes to raise $500.00 and sent the money to Robinson. (A few years later when Coffey went to get his air transport and instrument ratings from the government, the Commerce Department flight examiner recognized Coffey. The examiner was the man who had bought the Great Lakes from Coffey and had learned to fly in it! Needless to say, Coffey was awarded his air transport with instrument ratings.)

A young black man in uniform who felt very old and tired for his thirty-one years, boarded the North German Lloyd Lines passenger ship *Europa* bound for New York.

As the *Europa* plowed its way across the Atlantic toward America, the tension of the past year began to ebb slowly from him like ice melting in the first warm of spring. John realized how very tired he was and how much he wanted to go home.

Before boarding the *Europa* in England, John acquired back issues of the *London Times*. Each morning after breakfast he stretched out in his deck chair and read through them.

There were many items of interest, events that had occurred during the last month of Ethiopia's struggle to remain free. Germany had launched the giant 800-foot-long zeppelin Hindenburg on its first flight. It was to service a route from Germany to the United States. In England the new ocean liner *Queen Mary* was preparing for her maiden voyage to the United States. She would compete with the new French liner, *Normandy*. President Franklin D. Roosevelt was campaigning for re-election. His wife, Eleanor, had christened the new queen of the United States fleet, the aircraft carrier *Yorktown*, on April eighth. It was equipped with the navy's first line fighter, the already obsolete Gruman F3F bi-plane—Germany's Messerschmitt ME 109 and Britain's Spitfire were already flying at the time. There was a feature about a parade in Atlanta, honoring the Confederate veterans of the War between the States. More than a hundred of the veterans took part in the parade. One group in the same parade got a great deal of press—the Klu Klux Klan marched down Peachtree Street wearing satin hoods and robes. On the same page the *London Times* reported a mob shooting a Negro in Georgia and a lynching occurring in Arkansas.

As John read through the stack of newspapers, the stories dealing with world events and politics formed a picture of entangled nations stumbling toward armed conflict, seemingly blind to the horror that modern warfare had just demonstrated in Africa. He felt helpless as if he were in a dream.

The atmosphere on board ship was light, mostly conversations about fashion, sports, or business. When the possibility of war was mentioned, it was usually dismissed by the statement "War seems to be inevitable," always stated in a way, it appeared to John, as though the speaker had the impression the "inevitable war" would be somehow remote from his own nation, or that, at any rate, if it did affect his nation, the speaker's country would surely win and come out the better for it.

He also began to see why the League of Nations had done little to stop the war in Ethiopia and why that tribunal was now falling apart. France protested that Hitler was moving troops into the demilitarized Rhineland, in violation of the Locarno Treaty under which Germany, France, and Belgium had promised not to attack each other. Under the terms of the Locarno Treaty, England and Italy were jointly given the responsibility of enforcing the treaty should any of the three main parties violate it. However the two nations responsible for enforcing peace between Germany and France were now at odds with one another. As John read the news, he realized why England, sympathetic to Ethiopia, had disappointed those who felt she should have strongly aided Haile Selassie. Britain held vast interest in the Anglo-Egyptian Sudan and was nervous, fearing Italy would interfere with the critical water supply to her territory in the Sudan and to Egypt since Italy had captured land near Lake Tana, the source of the Blue Nile.

In Spain the last election had placed the government in the hands of a coalition of Socialist and leftist radicals who were stripping the church and the military of their traditional power. It appeared certain that leaders in the army were planning to rebel against the leftist government.

Japan, which had invaded northern China, was fighting Russia over Manchukuo, a land they disputed.

One article noted that the fall of Ethiopia marked, at long last, the total conquest of Africa by European nations that had begun in the sixteenth century.

Students throughout the United States staged demonstrations pledging not to support the United States government in any war it might conduct. President Franklin D. Roosevelt, speaking in his campaign for re-election, said that the United States would not increase its arms supply and intended to stay out of any war.

Organized crime was in the news too. Crime boss "Lucky" Luciano was going to jail, convicted on a charge of pandering.

Colonel Charles Lindbergh, who with Harry Guggenheim had recently pledged funds to aid a Dr. Robert Goddard with rocket experiments in New Mexico, was being criticized for remarking that the United States had better stay out of any conflicts with Germany. He had just returned from a personal tour of the new German airforce and said that America and the rest of the world had nothing to compare with it.

John stopped reading. He found he did not want to catch up on any more of world news. What it made clear to him was that the whole world was heading where he had already been—to war.

During the voyage home, he did not sleep well, waking often not knowing if he had screamed in his dream or out loud. He dreamed of bombings and of animals eating the unburied dead. He dreamed of flying in clouds knowing at any second he would feel the plane hit an unseen mountain ridge. He lay awake thinking of his friends who had died and wondering what would happen to those still living. In the mornings he would get up feeling tired and sick.

John knew he was a curiosity among his fellow passengers. He was black, and he was returning from "that Italian thing in Africa." On one occasion he overheard someone say, "He's a nigger aviator, I swear to God," followed by laughter which died down when the group of young Americans saw him approaching.

At his table in the dining salon everyone was polite. Someone would occasionally ask his opinion on an issue being discussed but usually he preferred to remain silent. Of the non-American passengers, the British seemed most interested in him. The Germans aboard ship ignored him except for two men, slightly younger than John, who asked if he would join them for a drink. They introduced themselves as members of the advance party for the zeppelin Hindenburg which would be making regular commercial runs between Germany and the United States. They were on their way to Lakehurst, New Jersey, they said, and were interested in hearing about the flying and bombing tactics used by the Italians in Ethiopia. John stood up, faced them and said, "Heil Hitler!" Both Germans, taken by surprise, clicked their heels and repeated, "Heil Hitler!" John walked to the ship's rail, saying to them over his shoulder. "Both you boys are Nazis, I see." The Germans looked at one another, but before they could speak John continued, "What would your Hitler fellow think if he found out a colored man was teaching a couple of his boys something? That might ruin his whole image."

One of the Germans interrupted him, "Don't be so rude, we are just flyers and offered you a drink to talk about flying."

"I've been bombed, gassed, and shot at by Fascists for a year. You'll have to excuse me if I'm not ready to sit down and drink with two more just yet." John turned and walked away.

He wondered how many more of the ship's crew were Nazis. There was an older German couple at his assigned dining table. They had been pleasant but there was an unmistakable arrogance among many of the younger Germans he found worrisome. In expressing their growing national feelings they came across more like bragging bullies than proud patriots.

Later that evening an Englishman walked up to Johnny. "Look here," he said, "I hope you don't think me rude, but I couldn't help but overhear what you said to the two German fellows up on the deck this afternoon. You are the American chap that flew Emperor Selassie, aren't you?"

"Yes, I was over there."

The Englishman replied, "I admire the way you gave those fellows what for. I thought, perhaps, you might consider having a drink or two with me and a couple of your countrymen over there." He motioned to a table where two men sat talking. "I'm afraid I told them about this afternoon, but they won't embarrass you with any questions if you don't want to talk about it. Besides, we can't talk much about our business either, except to say my work in England and theirs in America concerns building aircraft."

John thought for a moment and then said, "To tell you the truth, it's been a lonely trip; I think I might like to join you."

"Right. I'll introduce you and we'll fetch you a drink."

The Englishman was true to his word. No questions were asked unless John mentioned something about the war first, which he occasionally did during the evening. John learned that the two Americans, one from Texas, and the other from Massachusetts, worked for a young aircraft company called North American. The Englishman was with the British Air Purchasing Commission. That is all John learned about them as they talked into the night. They exchanged flying stories, particularly humorous ones. John found he could still laugh and was glad for the company, the refreshments, and the stories. After he got to bed that night—rather, early the next morning—he slept well for the first time in many months. He awoke at noon and was surprised to find himself feeling fit and hungry. "God knows where the world's headed," he thought to himself as he dressed, "but I'm going home." He wanted a rest, time to sort things out. For a while yet he was not going to get it.

# New York Loves a Hero

On the morning of May 18, 1936, the shoreline of America was clearly visible from John's ship. He got up late, shaved, put on a pair of slacks, a shirt and his leather flying jacket. It was a cool morning with a fair breeze blowing off the Atlantic. He walked forward toward the bow to watch the oncoming New York shoreline. The *Europa* was to ease from Lower Bay into the Narrows to pass through a quarantine inspection, then across Upper Bay into the Hudson and finally into its berth at the North German Lloyd's docks. It was not unusual for a few news reporters to board an incoming luxury liner down the bay, along with the quarantine officials, to sniff out a story concerning some movie star, socialite, or other important passenger aboard.

But while the ship was at quarantine that morning, nearly two dozen reporters flooded on board ignoring the stars and celebrities. Instead they thronged into the long corridors and public rooms of the ocean liner in search of a thirty-one-year-old black man they called the "Brown Condor of Ethiopia." They did not find him in his cabin. A small army of porters and stewards was enlisted to scour the ship in search of Colonel John C. Robinson. He was finally located, a solitary-looking figure, leaning against the ship's rail gazing at the towering skyline of Manhattan.

He looked curiously at the group rushing down the deck toward him and was startled when they identified themselves as representing various news services from throughout the country. Flash bulbs went off as photographers took pictures of a handsome young man wearing a leather flying jacket bearing the wings of the Imperial Ethiopian Air Corps and the Royal Lion of Judah, both insignia worked onto the jacket from woven threads of Ethiopian gold.

The reporters quickly ushered John off to the first-class saloon to get the "real low down" from the American hero of the Italo-Ethiopian War. At first embarrassed by being thrust into the center of attention, John suddenly recalled that this was what had taken him to Ethiopia in the first place: the chance to gain favorable publicity, which would aid Negroes to enter the field of aviation. Quiet by nature, he nevertheless determined to answer every question with careful consideration and courtesy. By the time the interview was finished, most of the passengers had departed the ship and were already making their way through customs inspection.

As he started down the gangplank, John, as well as two thousand fellow passengers and the hundreds of relatives and friends who had come to meet them, was amazed by a huge roar from the crowd waiting on the docks just clear of the custom area. Suddenly a forest of little Ethiopian and American flags began to flutter among the unusually large crowd. A group of young Ethiopian officers and embassy staff members burst into a patriotic song barely audible above the cheers from the crowd.

The demonstration interrupted the processing of the passengers and the unloading of the ship. Surveyor Thomas B. Terhune, in charge of the customs inspectors, gave orders that Colonel John Robinson be cleared as soon as possible so he would be free to meet the hundreds who waited to greet him. The customs inspector assigned to search his baggage asked a few perfunctory questions and then smiled as he said, "Glad to see you back, Colonel," and shook the flyer's hand.

As soon as he cleared customs, four large citizens from Harlem lifted John onto their shoulders. The crowd gave out a tumultuous roar. He was carried to the waiting room the North German Lloyd Line had quickly set aside so the hero could personally greet the hundreds who had come from all over the metropolitan area to bid him welcome. Ironically, the bewildered porter trailing behind the surging crowd with John's baggage was a recently immigrated Italian. After a time the crowd fell silent long enough for John to make a modest speech in which he thanked them for their rousing welcome.

Nothing would do but that John, luggage and all, be lifted onto the shoulders of the crowd and carried down to the street below where pandemonium again broke loose. People shouted, car and taxi horns blew, and John could do little except smile and wave at the mobs of people around him. He recognized a few friends in the crowd but they seemed unable to reach him. Finally Dr. P.M.W. Savory, chairman of New York's United Aid for Ethiopia, and several members of his committee, came to the colonel's aid, helping him get through the throng to the waiting limousine they had arranged for him. Safely seated in the black sedan, they left the cheering crowds behind. John, totally exhausted, sank back into the seat and took a deep breath. "Man, that was as scary as being caught in a bombing raid."

Dr. Savory said, "Well, Colonel, I'm afraid you had better become accustomed to a little of that. You have become a hero, and for a while at least, you'll receive a lot of attention. There will be a banquet in your honor tonight, but right now I know you need a little peace and quiet. I'll drop you off at your hotel. Your room is full of messages but you can deal with them tomorrow."

What Savory did not tell John was that a few community and business leaders had discovered his lack of finances and had set about to correct the situation. They had arranged a speaking tour not only in New York, but in Chicago and Detroit as well. Dining halls were made available free of charge. Black funeral homes furnished as many as twenty limousines at a time for parades. The price of a banquet ticket covered the cost of food with plenty left over for a fund for John. Everywhere he spoke there would be standing-room crowds only. He was a celebrity, a national hero with an audience in every major city asking to hear his story. But at the moment, John knew nothing of this.

As the long black La Salle made its way through New York's traffic toward Harlem, a thousand thoughts raced through his mind: the excitement of the welcome and of being back in the United States, the thought of having to make public appearances, and of wondering when he would ever get home to see his parents. The streets of New York seemed busy and happy, very far from the broken world he'd left behind in Ethiopia. There was little evidence of concern about the crumbling peace in Europe.

He found his hotel suite in Harlem filled with flowers, baskets of fruit, messages and bottles of champagne. He thanked his host, closed the door, ignored the champagne and poured himself a generous measure from a bottle of bourbon he found among the gifts. He turned on the faucets in the bathtub, filling it until it reached the overflow drain, then he lowered his aching body, bruised from having been carried, pulled and tossed about by the crowd, into the steaming, wonderful water. He leaned back, took a sip from the glass of bourbon and let the hot water drive all the tension from his body and thoughts from his mind.

The phone was ringing, at first far away, then suddenly it seemed loud and very near. He awoke with a start, not sure where he was. The room was dark but he could hear the noise of street traffic somewhere below. The phone beside the bed rang again. Finally finding it in the dark, he grasped the tall stand with the mouthpiece and lifted the receiver to his ear.

"Hello," he said.

"Hello, is this Colonel Robinson?"

"Yes."

"This is Dr. Savory. I'm down in the lobby. We have your car waiting."

John found the lamp switch and sat up on the edge of the bed. He was naked except for a towel tucked around his waist. "I'm just getting dressed, Doctor. To tell you the truth, the phone woke me up but I can be down in fifteen minutes. I'm sorry, will it make us late?"

"Not at all. There is plenty of time. By the way, how are you going to dress?"

"I bought a dark suit in London."

"I wonder if you would mind wearing your uniform. It's what the people expect to see. You are their hero and I think they would like to see the colonel in uniform."

John felt embarrassed. "I'm no hero, Doctor. I just wanted to prove a Negro could be a good pilot." There was a marked silence on the other end of the line. "If you feel wearing my uniform will help, I'm obliged to wear it. I'm really a little nervous about tonight. I mean I don't have a speech or even any notes."

He heard Savory laugh on the other end of the line. "You sure beat all, as they say, Colonel. You go halfway around the world to fly for an emperor, get shot at and make world headlines, then you come home and get nervous over accepting credit from your people. Everything will be fine. You won't need a speech, they just want to hear a few words from you and thank you for what you have done. Take your time. I'll be in the lobby. It's your night, Colonel Robinson."

John hung up the receiver and placed the phone back on the bed table. "Momma, you ought to see your boy now." He started to get up, stopped, picked up the phone and asked to be connected to Western Union. "I want to send a telegram to Mr. and Mrs. C. C. Cobb, please, 1905 Thirty-first Avenue in Gulfport, Mississippi." He sent a message home telling his mother he had several meetings in New York and Chicago and that he would be in Gulfport in a couple of weeks. He said he would write details, told her not to worry, and sent his love. Then he dressed in his uniform, picked up his hat, checked himself in the mirror, and said, "Well, here we go, ready or not."

At the banquet John was greeted by Dr. William Jay Schieffelin, Chairman of the Board of Trustees of Tuskegee Institute, and Claude A. Barnett, head of a large delegation from Chicago, which considered itself the hometown of Colonel Robinson. A great number of other civic and business leaders, black and white, also honored him. They gave speeches, which, in the words of one news article, "paid tribute to Colonel John Robinson's great contribution to Negro America."

When asked to speak, John thanked those listening for the honor they had given him. He then gave a brief account of the war, calling the Italian invasion and the mass slaughter of Ethiopians "a disgrace to civilization." He mentioned the courage of the loyal Ethiopian soldiers. He told of the problems these soldiers had faced not only from the Italians but from rebellious chiefs who had conspired with the Italians in hopes of getting power after the war. He ended by saying that Ras Desta and others would carry on guerrilla warfare from the mountains. He also told the banquet guests that all but three of the Ethiopian aircraft had been shot down or destroyed. John spoke very little about himself, admitting that he had been wounded and gassed.

The evening was the beginning of more than two weeks of banquets, parades, and meetings in New York and Chicago.

Lowell Thomas started a deluge of radio announce-
ments about him. So did the Trans-Radio Press, the
Mutual Broadcasting System, and the Press Radio News,
all sending out bulletins over both nationwide radio
networks. Newspapers throughout the country carried
such headings as: "All New York Greets Pilot on
Arrival," "Newsmen Get Lowdown on African War from
Colonel John C. Robinson," "Pioneered in Aviation in
Chicago-Started Air School," "Colonel Robinson, Brown
Condor, Returns Home," "Gangway for the 'Brown
Condor'" "Crowds Wait on War Hero."

Chicago was determined to surpass New York in
"welcoming its favorite son." John flew to Chicago on
an airline "escorted" by a plane piloted by Dr. Earl
Renfroe, the "flying colored dentist."

The Associated Press release told of hundreds of
Negroes breaking police lines to surround Robinson's
plane. Girls, members of the Challenger Air Pilots Association John had organized in 1932, presented him with
bouquets of flowers. Officers of the Eighth Infantry of
the Illinois National Guard; members of the United Aid
for Ethiopia; leaders and dignitaries including Robert
Abbott, editor of the *Chicago Defender*; former Representative Oscar de Priest and W. T. Brown, Jr., whom the
news media listed as "Mayor of Bronzeville" took part
in Chicago's welcoming party. Using limousines borrowed from black undertakers, John's parade drew
crowds estimated at more than 20,000 people. John spoke
to them from the balcony of the Grand Hotel at the corner
of Fiftieth and South Park. He then attended a banquet
given in his honor at the Binga Bank Building. Three
thousand daily newspapers throughout the country
printed pictures and stories about the Brown Condor's
return.

In spite of all the attention, John retained his quiet,
almost shy manner. He felt truly honored and enjoyed

seeing his old friends. He smiled often and spoke wherever he was asked but he was tired. He found himself saying the same things over and over. His audiences wanted to hear about the war, and about how he was wounded, and how he flew to escape the Italian planes, and these were the things he wanted least to talk about.

He learned what all men discover who have witnessed tragedy and faced hardship and who have survived when at times they thought they might not. There is no way to convey to others what it is really like: how it feels to be shot at, to fly through a storm, seeing a wall of solid rock just in time to avoid it, and then, safe on the ground, not talking about it except to laugh, feeling alive and discovering that a simple meal cooked over a small fire under a straw roof in the rain suddenly becomes the best-tasting meal you can ever remember. Or the way you react when the news comes that another friend won't ever come back. At first you hardly acknowledge that you've received the message. You act too busy to dwell on it and at the moment it might be true that you are too busy. It has happened before, it is happening all around, it may happen to you. You go on with your work. And then days later, slowly, heavily, you realize that what it really means is that you will never share the gift of your friend's unique company, or experience again his smile, voice, handshake, the simple treasures of his fellowship.

And how do you explain the horror, the terror, the fear you felt? How do you explain that all of that occurs either before, in dread anticipation, or after, in remembrance, but not during the events themselves, for during the events, things happen too fast, and you are too caught up in them to think in terms of horror or fear? How do you show someone who has not lived these things? How do you describe the smell of burning flesh?

How do you explain what it is like to scoop up a fallen child from the street while you are running for your life and only when you are safe realize that the child lost a foot in the bombing raid or has bled to death while you were running with it in your arms?

After the first news reporter interviewed him and after his first speech, John knew he could not make those who had not lived these things understand them; nor he thought, could anyone make people understand what war is unless they have lived it. Maybe that is why wars keep happening, he thought, why some new leader can always talk a new generation into war. They don't forget what the last war was like—they can't, they never knew in the first place.

He was grateful when the banquets and parades were over. He had refused no invitation but he had been uncomfortable. He had wanted to talk about opportunities for blacks in aviation but his audiences only wanted to hear of the war.

He had heard more news about Ethiopia since his arrival in New York. Three days after his own departure, the emperor had left Addis Ababa. Ras Desta was still fighting but the Italians had hunted down his sons and executed them. Mussolini had appointed Marshall Graziani as Viceroy of Ethiopia. Ordering all rebels shot, Graziani had the head of the Coptic Church executed. After an attempt on his life was made, he allowed hundreds of Blackshirts and Libyan *askaris* (native colonial soldiers from the Italian colony, Libya) to embark on a systematic massacre of the Ethiopians, setting native houses on fire with gasoline and then shooting the inhabitants as they fled the flames. The hate riot was allowed to go on for three days.

The emperor fled to Jerusalem hoping to establish his government in exile. Word reached John that Selassie could not set up permanent quarters there, however, because the Arabs and the Jews were fighting in the streets of the holy city, and the British were hard-put to stop it.

It was June, 1936 and the world was already beginning to forget troubled Ethiopia—its attention was now focused on a civil war in Spain.

# A Long Way Home

With the funds raised during his speaking tour John, with his partner Cornelius Coffey, put his flying school back in business. A new economical training plane was on the market. It was a Cub and it sold for $1,668.00. The partners paid $668.00 down and were in business again. In 1936, the Cub cost $1.98 an hour to operate including gas, oil, hangar rent, and insurance. They paid off the $1,000.00 balance owed on the Cub in six months.

John's business was in order. His immediate obligations to the many groups who had sponsored him (or whose cause his appearances and speeches could further) were fulfilled. He was tired. He thought of his parents, the house he had grown up in, the good smells of his mother's kitchen, the town in which he had spent his boyhood.

John was going home, and in style. There was enough money to make a down payment on a brand new SR-7 "gull-winged" five-place Stinson Reliant. Before putting it into service with the school he took off and pointed her nose southward. There would be several speeches to make on the way, but at last he was going home to Gulfport.

He was very pleased with his new NC 16161. The blue and grey highwing monoplane was the first of the popular Stinson Reliant models to employ the graceful "gull" wing, tapered upward slightly at the fuselage then outward. It had lovely elliptical lines that gave it the appearance of a seagull in gliding flight.

The founder of the Stinson company had been another Southern boy who had fallen in love with flying in his childhood and had never waivered from his intention to spend his life in or around airplanes. John knew that Eddie Stinson had done just that. From barnstormer to designer to head of Stinson Aircraft, he had left his mark in the field of aviation. The Stinson Company had become a part of the Cord Corporation of Chicago that manufactured Auburn automobiles, American-built Dusenberg automobiles, and Lycoming airplane engines. In 1934 at age thirty-eight, Eddie Stinson died of injuries received in a plane crash, but his company lived on and John was flying its newest plane.

He had chosen it because it could suit so many roles. It could carry five passengers in a comfortable, heated, sound-cushioned cabin. With the seats removed he could carry cargo. It was easy enough to fly so that he could use it for training new pilots. It had an electric starter, cruising at 145 mph and with a fuel capacity of 76 gallons, its 250 hp Lycoming engine would carry it 600 miles without refueling. John was proud of it.

Lake Michigan and the sprawling metropolis of Chicago slipped away behind him. He felt happy and relaxed. He was where he loved to be most, alone in the sky with all the earth spread out before him.

Cruising at 4,000 feet he spotted a formation of five bi-planes, tiny specks in the sky off his right wing. For a moment the chill of war returned. His palms began to sweat. Then he remembered there were no enemy aircraft in the peaceful skies of America. He was right. The planes were military but they continued on their way, a training flight of four students and one instructor. "You best settle down there, Colonel. You're home now, boy," he said out loud to himself. He relaxed surrounded by the steady rhythmic sounds of the Lycoming radial and the faint odor of warm engine oil blended with the sweet smell of the new fabrics and leather of his aircraft's cabin.

Three hours later he landed for fuel at Cairo where Illinois, Kentucky, and Missouri meet at the junction of the Ohio and Mississippi Rivers. After helping fuel his Stinson, he bought a soft drink and package of Ritz crackers, the classic "pilot's lunch."

From Cairo John followed the Mississippi. The corn fields along the river delta of Illinois and Missouri gave way to cotton fields as he followed the "Mighty Muddy" southward toward Memphis. An hour-and-a-half later he turned southeastward over Memphis and began following the highway leading toward Birmingham. The paved highways of Illinois had given way to Tennessee's highways whose paved sections were broken by long stretches of gravel roads. South of Memphis, Mississippi's gravel highways were for the first time beginning to show the efforts of a new paving program just begun by Mississippi's new governor, Hugh White. It would be years before a paved highway would run all the way from Memphis to the coast.

John had three stops to make before heading for Gulfport: Birmingham for fuel, Tuskegee where he would spend the night and address the students of his alma matter, and Meridian where he had agreed to make a brief speech before continuing home.

When he landed at Birmingham he noticed the looks on the faces of a small group of men who came out of the flight line shack behind the fuel pumps. He knew well what had caused their surprise. It wasn't the new plane, though the group had seen the Stinson land and had come out to take a closer look. He knew it had to be the first gull-winged Stinson they had ever seen, but the real surprise came when John opened the cabin door and climbed down. He overheard one of the group say, "I'll be damned, I ain't never seen a nigger flying before." Another man wearing a flying jacket stepped forward.

"That's a fine looking machine. Do you mind if I have a closer look at it."

John asked, "Can I get the tanks topped and the oil checked?" The man in the flying jacket turned to the half dozen "airport regulars" standing behind him. "Henry, fill her up and check the oil." A young black man in coveralls said, "Yes, sir, Mr. Hayes," and moved over to a pump marked Shell Aviation. Hayes turned to John and asked, "Your name happen to be Robinson?"

"Yes, that's right."

"You the one that just got back from Ethiopia and the Italian war there?"

"Yes, I was there."

"I've read about you," the man offered his hand to John. "I'm Hayes," he said. "This is my flight operation. Could you use a cup of coffee?"

"That would be fine," John replied, following Hayes past the onlookers toward the small frame office building some twenty yards beyond the fuel pump.

A cup of coffee later, John paid his bill, used the restroom behind the office and walked out to the plane where onlookers were still gathered. "It's a beautiful plane you got there," one of them said.

"Thank you, it's a good ship," John replied. He answered a few other questions about the plane while he climbed up to check the fuel and oil filler caps. He then checked the fuel strainers and climbed into the cabin. "Stop in again," called Hayes who had come out to the plane with him. John waved and called, "Clear," to warn that he was going to start the engine. The electric starter slowly turned the prop. After a couple of revolutions, the engine fired and roared into life. He waved again and Hayes nodded. The small group watched the blue Stinson lift off and turn to the southeast.

Then they filed into the office shack. "Well, that was something," one of the group said. Another walked over to the coffee pot. Two cups from a rack of mugs sat on the desk with a little coffee left in them. "Dammit, Hayes, did you let that nigger drink out of my cup?"

Hayes looked at him. "No, I used your cup. He drank out of mine. I'll tell you another thing. That 'nigger', as you put it, is Emperor Haile Selassie's personal pilot. He's just been through a war in Africa, and from what I've read in the news, I'd lay money he could fly rings around your dumb ass." The rest of the group thought that was funny.

Hayes walked out of the office and saw the young man in overalls still looking toward the sky where John's plane was a tiny speck, barely visible. "Henry," called Hayes, "you been doing a good job around here since you started last month. I guess maybe you've earned yourself a plane ride. You want one?" The young man broke into a wide grin.

"Yes, sir, Mr. Hayes. I been wanting one since the first day I come out here. That's why I asked you fo' a job."

Hayes said, "Well, go climb up in front of that Waco, we'll take her around the field a couple of times."

Henry ran out to the bi-plane. "I told my daddy I'd git a ride but he won't believe it."

"If you can find your house, we'll fly over it and you can wave to him," Hayes replied as he helped fasten the safety harness of a very happy, young black man.

In the late afternoon sunlight, John's graceful Stinson circled the campus at Tuskegee, settling gently on a field nearby. Shortly afterwards, several automobiles pulled to a stop. From one of them two men walked toward John, who was standing beside his plane. The first was an old friend of John's, Captain A. J. Neely, the college registrar. Behind him was President Patterson, head of Tuskegee.

"Welcome home, Colonel Robinson. We are very proud to have you with us again," said Patterson.

"Thank you, sir. I feel at home here."

Neely said, "John, a room at my home is ready for you. We thought you might like to clean up before we have supper at President Patterson's home.

"After supper the teachers and staff would love to meet you. Tomorrow we thought you could address the students at the summer session. Then the people at Meridian want us to call and let them know when you will be there."

"I'm afraid we have a lot planned for you, Colonel. I hope you don't mind too much," added Patterson.

John smiled, "I've about gotten used to it. To tell the truth, supper sounds fine. Since breakfast this morning in Chicago, I've only had a few crackers and a Coca-Cola."

"Well, John, we didn't plan a fancy meal. We decided fried chicken, field peas, candied yams, and apple pie might sound good to someone who had been away from the South for as long as you have."

"Captain Neely," John replied, "those Italians must have killed me after all cause it sounds like I've died and gone to heaven. Now if you tell me I can have hot buttered grits and biscuits with breakfast in the morning, I'll know it's true." They all laughed and started for the car.

The *Tuskegee Messenger* reported at great length about the visit of "one of the boys enrolled at Tuskegee in the early twenties" who now returned as a celebrity. Recounting John's appearance before the student body, the newspaper stated, "In presenting Colonel Robinson, President Patterson referred with pride to the fine record of this Tuskegee graduate in blazing the trail for Negro youth in a new field of endeavor and proving to the world beyond doubt the Negro's capacity for accuracy, endurance, skill and courage."

The article ended by saying, "A course of instruction in aeronautics is being planned by the department of mechanical industries at Tuskegee, and Mr. Robinson is scheduled to return as instructor in the course."

John knew things were not going to be quite that simple. After a long discussion with school officials during which he explained some of the requirements of setting up a school of aeronautics, he realized such a program was still a long way off. The school did not have the finances available. A school of aeronautics would require a shop and mechanical facilities, special tools, an aircraft, an airstrip, operating funds for the maintenance of the aircraft and salaries for a full-time aviation instructor and other personnel. What did happen as a result of the meeting was a firm commitment from Tuskegee to work toward the establishment of such a school.

He had one more stop to make, at Meridian in Mississippi, before taking a rest with his folks at Gulfport. The air was clean and filled with white fluffs of summer clouds as John left Tuskegee behind in his Stinson. He flew across Montgomery and watched the curving path of the Alabama River wander along below, leading him to Selma on a westerly course across the state.

By the time he reached Demopolis, where the Black Warrior joins the Tombigbee River, flowing south towards Mobile Bay, John knew he'd had at least one cup of coffee too many at breakfast and decided to make an unscheduled rest stop. Just west of Demopolis he spotted a clear field alongside a gravel highway. The field was just behind what looked like a country store. It appeared level and clear. After making a low pass to check the field, John put the Stinson down.

Halfway through the landing roll, he felt a bump followed by a pull toward the right. He was rolling too slowly for the rudder to be effective in directional control so he applied gentle pressure to his left brake to keep the plane from ground looping. He climbed down from the cabin, knowing what the trouble must be. "Sure enough, it's flat as hell," he said to himself as he squatted down and looked under the plane's belly at the right tire. What was worse, he could see that the side wall of the tire was badly cut. It could not be patched.

John looked around. The store he had seen from the air was two hundred yards away. There was no traffic on the road. He stood up beside the plane, relieved himself and thought, "You just couldn't wait twenty-five more minutes. Fifty miles and you would be there. Son of a gun." Walking down the track his right wheel had made through the short grass, he found the cause of his cut tire. Lying a foot from where it had been torn from the ground was the dirt-encrusted, jagged top half of a broken gallon jug. "Hell of a way to waste mooonshine whiskey and airplane tires." He took off his uniform blouse (he had worn his uniform for his appearance at Meridian), slung it over the pilot's seat, and started for the store.

Most of the dark red paint had peeled off the pine-board siding of the store building. The structure was larger than it had first appeared. A wide porch ran across the width of the storefront, covered by a hip roof that extended out over a single gasoline pump. Several signs were nailed to the wall. The largest read "Coca-Cola." A cardboard poster advertised Wings cigarettes and beside it a handmade sign read "For sale, 29 Model A, Runs, $25.00."

John walked up the well-worn wooden steps and opened the screened front door. Inside was one naked light bulb burning over the center counter. There were no windows on the sides of the building. A large electric fan, installed in a vent cut through the roof, hummed noisily overhead. An elderly man dressed in khaki pants and shirt, and wearing a white bib apron was sitting on a stool working on a stack of invoices. The man looked up and eyed John. "Morning, I didn't hear you drive up. You need some gas or you want something in here?"

"I don't have a car. I need to use a telephone. Do you have one?"

"Yep, we got the only one within three miles. Where you from? I don't believe I seen you around here before. You say you walked here?"

"Well, I didn't walk here, exactly. I flew." The man looked up at John, who quickly added, "My plane is in the pasture back of here."

"The hell you say. You trying to fool with me?"

"You can see the plane if you look out back there."

The storekeeper had become very suspicious. "You mean you landed an airplane behind my store?"

"You can see it from the edge of the front porch," John said walking ahead of the man, who followed him out on the porch.

The store owner looked around the building, "Well, I'll be damned." He walked back into the store. "I thought I heard a motor a while ago, but I walked out front and didn't see a car on the road. You got some kind of trouble? Where do you want to call?"

"I landed to take a rest, and I cut a tire. I'd like to call the airfield at Meridian. I'm gonna need a new tire."

"That'll be all right but the operator will have to let me know how much to charge you." He walked over to the telephone hanging on the post by his desk. It was a cranktype phone. He picked up the ear piece and listened for a moment. "Say, Mrs. Hinton, this is George Thornton, yes, ma'am, at the store. I wonder if ya'll would mind letting me have this line. I got a fellow here who landed an airplane. He's a colored fellow too. That's right, a colored fellow. Yes ma'am. I sure will." He paused and then turned to John. "We got a six-party line on this thing." He then turned the crank on the side of the phone box. "Operator, who's this, Mary? Mary, I got a fellow here at the store that wants to call Meridian. When he gets through, I need to know how much to charge him. That's right." He turned to John. "Here you go, just tell her who you want."

"Thank you." John took the receiver and asked the operator to connect him with anyone at the airport in Meridian. After a pause, a lot of clicking noises, and a conversation between operators, John was told to "Go ahead, please, the airport is on the line."

"Hello, I'd like to speak to someone from the flying service, please."

The voice on the other end of the line said, "I'm Al Key, what can I do for you? Can you speak louder, I can hardly hear you?"

"Mr. Key, I'm John Robinson. I'm over here near Demopolis. I blew a tire on a Stinson and I wonder if someone over there can get me some help. I'll need a new tire."

"Are you the Robinson that flew in Ethiopia? Supposed to make some kind of speech here today?"

"Yes, I am." John then asked, "Are you one of the Key brothers that set the world endurance record?"

"That's right. Look, there must be a thousand colored folks out here at the field already. I'll come over and get you. If you can get your wheel off, we'll get it fixed here while you make your talk, and then get you and the wheel back to your plane. That sound O.K.?"

"Mr. Key, that would be mighty fine. Just a minute and I'll get Mr. Thornton here to tell you exactly where we are."

"Tell him you are at Thornton's store on Highway 80, four miles east of the Tombigbee bridge."

John relayed the directions to Al Key. Then he borrowed a screwtype jack from the storekeeper and returned to the plane to remove the right wheel.

Afterwards he went back to the store where he bought a quart of milk and a box of salt crackers for lunch and sat out on the porch talking with Thornton until they heard the sound of an aircraft overhead. By the time they walked out to the pasture, Al Key was waiting for them beside his Curtiss plane.

A year earlier, Al Key and his brother Fred had set a world endurance record flying the modified Curtiss monoplane. Using inflight fueling and supply methods of their own design, they remained airborne for over twenty-seven days!

The two Mississippians stood for a moment looking at one another. "Mr. Key, I'm John Robinson. I sure thank you for taking the time to help me. I would be in a devil of a mess without you."

"Well, let's get that tire fixed. Besides, I think every black from Meridian and surrounding parts must be waiting for you at the airport."

John thanked Mr. Thornton and told him he would return his jack after they brought the new tire back. He and Al Key climbed into the Curtiss.

A half hour later they approached the airfield at Meridian, named Key Field in honor of the two brothers. Years later Al Key described their arrival:

> We circled over the field and could see the crowd waiting on the ramp. There were about four thousand people. In those days we weren't so concerned about regulations. I checked the area and saw no other traffic. Robinson looked at me and I just smiled and pointed at the crowd. Then I put the plane in a shallow dive to pick up lots of speed. We flew down between the terminal building and the hangar, and I pulled the Curtiss right up and over into an Immelmann turn. Later, one of the boys on the ground swore to me that the whole crowd went wild and that an old colored man standing near him hollered out loud, "Look at

that nigger fly!" In any case when we came in and landed, I let Robinson get out and I sort of stayed hidden in the plane. After I had done the Immelmann, he had looked over and laughed, shaking his head, but he didn't say anything. Later, after he'd made his speech, we took the new tire and flew back to pick up his plane. Just before I left him, we shook hands and he thanked me. Then he told me that all the blacks thought he had been flying and done that crazy stunt. I told him that we would leave it that way. He grinned and we shook hands again. I liked him. Yes, he was all right.

# Gulfport, 1936

Turning south over Meridian, John followed the gravel highway past Laurel and Hattiesburg. The last seventy miles from Hattiesburg to Gulfport seemed the longest. The late afternoon sun cast a yellowish hue on the earth below. A young forest was struggling to cover the scars left by the clear-cutting practices that had raped the area's virgin southern yellow pine over twenty years before.

Ahead, John saw a clean, distinct line just below the horizon. The sight filled him with the good, happy-tired feeling that comes at journey's end. The line was the Gulf of Mexico meeting America's southern border along the Mississippi coast. The gently rolling terrain changed to sandy pine-covered flat coastal plain as the blue Stinson flew the last few miles to the coast. Black smoke poured from the tall stack of the town's power plant on the beach at Thirtieth Avenue, making a smudge against the clean horizon of the Gulf. John flew over the huge wooden Great Southern Hotel and on out over the harbor. The great concrete steps of the seawall stretched east and west from the harbor down the shoreline for miles. Palm trees grew in the broad neutral grounds that ran down the center of several of Gulfport's streets.

"It's pretty," John thought to himself, "but it sure seems smaller." He circled over the end of east pier and saw that it was still a popular fishing spot. Men, women, and children, black and white, sat or stood along the end of the earth-filled pier, trying their luck. Some of the children were crabbing and several of them waved as John circled low overhead.

To the south he could see Cat Island and the silhouette of Fort Massachusetts on Ship Island, some twelve miles to the southeast. He looked down at the spot just east of the harbor where he had seen his first airplane. He vividly remembered seeing the old Curtiss pusher take off from the water. It seemed a long time and a million miles ago.

Just west of the harbor and the Gulf and Ship Island tracks, he turned north and flew toward the grass airfield. He looked down on the Big Quarter and saw the two-story house where he had grown up. He wondered if his sister, Bertha, would be home during his visit. Bertha had married a fellow schoolteacher, H. L. Stokes, and they were living in Arkansas.

John landed at the airport. There was one hangar, with half a dozen planes parked near it. The only regular flight which used the field was a mail plane. Air mail service in Gulfport had begun in the late twenties. But there was enough local and transient flying to keep Arthur Hughes, who had been running the airport since 1934, busy. He gave John a ride to his mother's house.

In answer to the knock on her front door, Celest Cobb came from the back of the house, wiping her hands on her apron. Through the screen door she saw a tall man in uniform. He had a mustache.

"Hi, Momma."

The small stout woman stopped at the door. She held both hands to her lips. "Johnny! Oh praise Jesus!" She threw open the door and put her arms around his neck. He picked her up off the floor and kissed her and swung her around on the porch. "My Johnny! Daddy Cobb and me prayed so hard for you. We are so proud. Everybody's been waiting for you. We're all so proud of you, so thankful you're home." John put his arm around his mother and they walked into the house together.

They were sitting in the kitchen when they heard the front door open and the distinct step of a person walking with a limp. Celest motioned for John to be quiet and then said, "I'm in the kitchen. Did you bring home the fresh shrimp for the gumbo?" Mr. Cobb continued toward the kitchen. "Yes, honey, I got shrimp, fresh okra, and I also bought a basket of peaches and some fine pork chops." He rounded the kitchen doorway, "That boy is gonna need lots of your cooking when he gets . . ."

John stood up and grinned at the grey-haired man who had stopped in the doorway. "Hi, Daddy."

Charles Cobb set the bags of groceries on the kitchen table. "You look fine, son."

The older man fought to keep the tears of joy from welling up in the corners of his eyes. He stepped forward and held the son he loved so much. John noticed his dad seemed much older than he had remembered and that his limp had grown a little more pronounced than before. He put both arms around him saying, "You're looking great yourself," and for a moment held this gentle man he loved very tight.

That evening the Cobb home filled with friends and neighbors of all ages. Some brought food and drink, turning it into a neighborhood party. John saw friends from his Thirty-third Avenue school days. To his surprise a friend he had met in Chicago brought him a chocolate cake, his favorite dessert. She had been introduced to him while visiting Chicago but her home was actually Pass Christian, Mississippi, only a few miles down the beach. She was one of several young women who paid a great deal of attention to John.

Everyone wanted to hear about the war, Emperor Selassie, John's world travels, his battles with the Italian flyers, and how he was wounded. John told some stories and answered questions, passing lightly over as many as he could and trying to hide the embarrassment he felt from all the attention.

Leaders from the A.M.E. (African Methodist Episcopal Church) and from the Bethel Baptist Church said they hoped he didn't mind their having arranged a big day of events for him on Sunday. First, there would be a picnic at the airport where they hoped he would agree to give airplane rides. They would raffle off chances for the first ride. John looked at his beaming mother and told them he would be glad to do it. Sunday night there would be a big reception at the Bethel Baptist Church. They all agreed that would be wonderful and John realized that much planning had already been done.

He was told that the *Daily Herald* would like for him to call at their office for an interview. Several city officials, he learned had agreed to attend the gathering at the airport Sunday afternoon.

When the last neighbor had left, John let out an audible sigh and slumped into an overstuffed chair in the corner of the living room. His mother had gone upstairs to ready his room. Charles Cobb returned from the kitchen with two bottles of Dixie Beer. For a few minutes both men sat and sipped quietly.

Then Charles Cobb said, "You seem a little uneasy, son. I guess we're making too much fuss around here over you. Everyone wants to see you but I told your Momma you were gonna need some rest."

"Well, Daddy, it's really something to get the attention but it all gets pretty heavy. I want to talk about aviation—but everyone just wants to hear about the war. But they don't *really* want to hear about the war, I mean how it happened and why it's gonna happen again, soon I think, in Europe. People, black and white, ask me about how exciting it was, they want the thrills not the real details. I don't think I could tell them anyway. Not even you, Daddy. I've seen so much I don't want to talk about,

I don't think I can talk about. It'll just take me a while longer to settle down. I haven't had much time to rest." He took a sip of beer. "I'd be lying though if I said I didn't like getting the attention and meeting people and being looked up to. Right now it's nice being home."

"We're mighty glad you are home, son. I wish you would stay."

"I wish I could, but there's just no place for me in the South. It'll be a while before Tuskegee could have a place for me. Things are different in the North. Not everything. There are plenty of people up there who don't like colored people, just like there are plenty of people down here that have been good to us, but there is a hell of a lot more opportunity up there for a colored man with an education or a skill. I've taught as many white students to fly as I have colored, a lot more in fact. I just couldn't do that down here."

He didn't tell his stepfather that he also had learned to like a different lifestyle. He had been around the world. Among his friends were leaders of Ethiopia and the United States. On many occasions he had dined with the American and British ambassadors and he had many friends who were leaders in business or education in New York, Chicago, and other cities.

"Well, son, I understand. This has been a good place for your mother and me. It's for sure that everything's not right for colored folks, but I don't think we'd be happy anywhere else now. But we know you are used to a different way and you got things to do. I guess Chicago is more home to you now. Just know we love you and all your people are proud of you."

"I'm proud of you and Momma. You worked so hard to send me and Bertha to school. Ya'll are part of everything we do."

Mr. Cobb got up and put his hand on John's shoulder. "Come on, son. We must have worn you plumb out."

They walked up the stairs together.

"Speaking of your sister, she was sorry they couldn't come down for your homecoming."

"Well, I'll just have to fly up there and see them in Arkansas on the way back. Momma said they are doing real well."

"They're fine. Your Momma and me been mighty blessed by you children. You sleep late as you want. I've arranged to be off tomorrow afternoon. How long since you been fishing?"

"Lord, I don't know."

"The tide will be changing late afternoon."

"That sounds fine."

"Good. I got two poles and a bucket. We'll see if we can't fill it up with speckle trout for yo' Momma. Good night, son."

John woke the next morning feeling rested and at ease. It was nearly nine o'clock. Celest Cobb came into his room carrying the clean uniform she had unpacked, brushed and pressed. "Good morning, sleepyhead," she said. "I'll have you some breakfast by the time you git dressed. You s'posed to be at the newspaper by ten."

"I thought I would get out of that uniform while I'm home."

"Well, you gonna wear it to the newspaper and you got to wear it for the goings-on this Sunday. Besides, I took your suit to the cleaners and the rest of your things I'm washing."

"All right, Momma. I can see you haven't changed a bit," he laughed.

"That's right. You may be an emperor's pilot, but 'round here, I'm queen of this house."

"Yes, ma'am."

Before he had finished dressing, the wonderfully blended smell of fresh coffee and cooking bacon drifted up to him from the kitchen below. He put on his tie, buffed the toes of his shoes, and went down to a morning feast. Celest fussed over him, glowing with the joy of having her boy home. There was hot coffee to start things off. Then came two eggs over light, crisp bacon, steaming buttered grits, and biscuits with homemade scuppernong jelly. There was also a jar of pure cane syrup to be poured over a plate of hot biscuits, sliced open and buttered.

Finishing his last cup of coffee, John protested, "I think after all this breakfast, I'm gonna have to go back upstairs and take a little nap."

"You git yo'self out of this house and down to the paper. If you walk down there instead of ride'en you'll feel just right."

"All right, Momma, I'm going. I wanted to walk through town anyway. It's been a long time since I've seen it."

He left the house and walked toward town. He smiled to himself thinking about his mother. She seemed never to change, maybe she was a little heavier, but she was still her wonderful self. Daddy Cobb looked older, a little tired, thought John. Following the red-brick-paved street he soon reached the heart of the small downtown section. He noticed a new service station on the corner. "Another one with two gas pumps and three rest rooms," John thought to himself. On the side of the new station were two doors, one marked "Ladies," the other "Gentlemen." In the back John found another door. It was marked "Colored." The station attendant looked a little perplexed. He had never seen a Negro in an officer's uniform before.

At the corner John turned toward the train station.

"Johnny! Johnny Robinson," called a large man who had pulled to the curb in a Dodge touring car. John looked at the white man wearing a sailor straw hat. John recognized the smiling man as C. A. Simpson. He had worked for Simpson when he was in high school.

"Hello, Mr. Simpson, how have you been?"

"Just fine, Johnny. Mrs. Simpson's maid told her this morning that you had gotten home yesterday. You have really done yourself proud, Johnny. We read about you being in the war with the Italians. You have accomplished a great deal, John, several men including the mayor were talking about it this morning. Do you need a ride somewhere?"

"Thank you, Mr. Simpson, I appreciate it but I've just got a few blocks to go. I'd sort of like to look the town over."

"All right, Johnny, just want you to know we think a lot of you."

From the corner of the street John could see the train station where the G & SI tracks running south to the port crossed the east-west tracks of the L & N. It did not seem as busy a place as it once had been. The buildings across the street from the station looked worn, especially the small brick hotel. When he reached the station he walked around the platform to the Railway Express freight room. A stout black man, slightly younger than John, was loading cartons onto a pushcart. He was wearing railroad bib overalls and a seasoned railroad cap. A watch chain hung down from one pocket while from the center pocket of his bib, the draw string of a tobacco bag showed he was a "roll your own" smoker.

"Can you tell me when the next train for New Orleans leaves?"

The man looked up at John. He put down the package he was holding and broke into a wide grin. "Johnny! Hot damn if you don't look like something, man! I mean you looking good." He shook John's hand and slapped him on the shoulder. "Come on, I want you to meet everybody. I been telling 'em all about you. You know I remember when you gave me your favorite kite. That was the best flying kite a kid ever had."

"I really only have time to say hello, Marcus. I've got to get down to the newspaper office. We'll get together later."

"Well, just let me introduce you to the fellows and the station master and my bossman."

He led John down the platform past the two waiting room doors, one marked "White Only", the other marked "Colored", and to the office window where a telegraph operator sat working his key. After he had been introduced to all the railroad men in sight he excused himself by inviting them all out to the airport on Sunday. The station master was promised a flight.

It was already ten o'clock and John quickened his step. Passing the Gulf "moving picture" theater near the corner, he saw that it had a side entrance blacks had to use to buy tickets and that they had to go upstairs to watch from the balcony. It and the Paramount theater were the only buildings in town cooled with "refrigerated air."

Turning down Fourteenth Street he walked four blocks to the *Daily Herald* Building. It was "Trade Day in Downtown Gulfport" and all the merchants had big sale signs in their windows. A grocery store had various prices painted on its front windows: steak, 23 cents a pound; lettuce, 5 cents a head; pork and beans, four cans, 19 cents; five bars of Octagon soap at 10 cents. Elmer's Department Store had a sale on men's summer clothes. Men's seersucker suits were $3.98; pants and shirts were a dollar; straw hats 79 cents. John needed new summer clothes and decided to buy some on the way home.

His interview in the newspaper made the front page of the Gulfport-Biloxi *Daily Herald*, the only daily on the coast. The headline stated, "Gulfport Negro Who Piloted Emperor Haile Selassie Visits Home; Relates His Experiences in Wartime Flying." The article, dated June 26, 1936, began:

> J. C. Robinson, Negro aviator who gained worldwide fame as Emperor Haile Selassie's official air pilot and who was in charge of the entire Ethiopian Air Force, is in Gulfport visiting his stepfather and mother, C. C. Cobb and wife who reside at 1905 Thirty-first Avenue. Robinson called at *The Herald* Office this morning wearing the Ethiopian army official uniform. His rank is Colonel and his uniform carries the official emblem of the emperor, "The Lion of Judah", worked in gold mined from the gold mines of Ethiopia from which King Solomon was supposed to have secured much of the gold for his famous temple at Jerusalem.
>
> He was employed by C. A. Simpson in Gulfport at one time and went from Gulfport to Chicago where he worked for six years with the Curtiss Flying Service.
>
> Ethiopia had 24 airplanes during the war, he said, and all but three of them were shot down.
>
> During his thirteen month's service in the Ethiopian air service, he was wounded three times and gassed twice.

The article described the situation in Ethiopia and reported the emperor's escape. It concluded by stating that Robinson would make an appearance sponsored by church groups, before returning to Chicago in a few days.

Celest Cobb carefully clipped the article from the front page and placed it in the scrapbook with all the others she had collected. Then she put the book back on the table beside her Bible.

That Sunday the grounds of the Gulfport airfield were crowded with members of the town's black community. A sprinkling of whites were also present. Families were enjoying picnic lunches laid out on the ground. Children ran among the crowd, paying little attention to their mothers' warning not to "git yo' Sunday clothes dirty." Arthur Hughes patrolled the hangar, warning, "You young'uns stay off those airplanes and don't touch the propellers." He checked the switches on every plane again to make sure none had been turned on by curious little fingers. It was the largest crowd ever gathered at the airfield.

Cakes and cookies were being sold by the church groups. Several women walked through the crowd selling chances on the first plane ride with Colonel Robinson. Chairs had been put on the flat bed of a truck parked near the freshly washed blue and grey Stinson. It was used as a platform from which the leaders of the various groups made short speeches and announcements. Charles and Celest Cobb were introduced and given seats on the platform. Among the white citizens present was the mayor of Gulfport, J. W. Milner, and Dr. Dox, the president of Gulf Park College, an aviation buff who had introduced a course on flying instruction to the all-girl school.

After all the introductions were completed, John made a short speech, thanking those present for honoring him with such a homecoming. There was much applause repeated once again when the announcement was made that the drawing for the airplane ride was about to take place.

John reached into the hat box into which all the tickets had been placed. When he read the number of the winning ticket, there was a squeal from the crowd as a young woman ran forward holding the matching half of the ticket tightly in her hand. The crowd applauded again and then laughed as a man near the edge of the platform recognized the winner and called, "My goodness, Colonel Robinson, you be careful, that's my daughter!"

John smiled and said, "I certainly will, Mr. Gaston." The crowd standing around the Stinson parted to allow John and his passenger through. They watched with intense interest as the colonel made a last inspection of the craft before securing his excited passenger's seat belt and closing the cabin door. The onlookers moved away from the plane as the starter engaged the propeller with a whining noise. A cloud of blue smoke gushed from the radial engine's exhaust stack. The engine roared alive, blowing loose grass and sand at those who stood behind. Miss Gaston waved frantically at her friends while the plane taxied past them. The crowd moved to the edge of the runway and grew silent as John wheeled the plane into the wind. The engine thundered out its 250 hp, lifting the Stinson into the air well before it reached the people waving and clapping their hands. Several small boys ran along the ground chasing the graceful ship as it climbed toward the south. Still standing on the speaker's platform, tightly clutching the arm of Charles Cobb, Celest felt both immense pride and trembling fear as her son's plane roared past. C. C. Cobb put his arm around her and gently patted her shoulder.

John carried his passenger south over the shore then circled the town. A few minutes later he was back at the field. Before landing, he brought the plane down to fifty feet and made a long low pass down over the runway to the great pleasure of those gathered below. He then circled the field and brought the plane in, bouncing lightly once and quickly slowing the plane, before turning off the strip onto the parking area. John flew eager passengers all that afternoon, including Mayor Milner, Dr. Cox from Gulf Park College, and, late in the day, Mr. Gaston, whose daughter had won the first ride. Then he took his quietly terrified momma and his proud and thrilled daddy for a gentle flight at sunset.

Those who were there that day still remember it as a grand occasion, outdone, perhaps, only by the brief stop that year of the presidential train. On his short appearance and speech Franklin Roosevelt, who was campaigning for re-election, assured listeners in Gulfport that the nation's dreadful economic problems were being solved and that America would never become involved in the next war in Europe, should one occur.

# Hard Choices

By the summer of 1936 John, reunited with his partner Cornelius Coffey, moved the J. C. Robinson School of Aviation to the grounds of the Poro College in Chicago. The aviation school was established in the carriage house of a large Victorian mansion that stood on the Poro College property. John had been invited to move his school there by the remarkable founder of the college, Mrs. Annie E. Malone. She was the creator and owner of a very successful cosmetics company, the first to create beauty products specifically designed for Negro women. A pioneer in the field of black entrepreneurship, she recognized John's achievements and his ability to set an example for others. It is not unreasonable to also say that she, like most women of all ages who met him, was charmed by his sometimes daring yet always gracious manner.

The following summer, John, flying the Stinson, and Coffey, piloting the Taylorcraft, went on a barnstorming tour to promote their aviation school. On July 9, 1937 an article in a Kansas City paper described one of the promotional flights made by Robinson. Under the headline, "Colonel John C. Robinson Lands at Local Airport," the article read:

> Ambitious to make American Negro youth air-minded, Col. John C. Robinson, chief of Haile Selassie's air forces during the Italo-Ethiopian war, landed his five-passenger monoplane in the Kansas City municipal airport Sunday morning, July 4, to spend a few hours before continuing to Topeka where he spoke Sunday and Monday nights.

The grey and blue 1937 Stinson monoplane—NC 16161—hit the runway of the airport at exactly 11:50 Sunday morning.

Flying with the colonel were his two copilots, Frank Browning and Joe Muldrew, both of Chicago; Mrs. Annie E. Malone, head of the Poro College of Chicago; and Miss Yutha Tolson, Kansas Citian, who has been in Chicago several weeks taking a special course at the Poro College.

Robinson and his copilots are making a tour in the interest of Colonel Robinson's school of aviation in Chicago in which 50 students already are enrolled, 40 white and 10 Negro. Colonel Robinson believes that aviation is a field with a great future for young Negroes who are well trained in aeronautics.

At his school on the Poro College grounds in Chicago, established in September, 1936, half a dozen instructors are busy teaching youths flying from the bottom up.

The Brown Condor will be in Mound Bayou, Miss., for the fiftieth anniversary celebration July 11-17. After that he plans to tour the Southwest in the interest of his flying school.

John was building a profitable business in the risky field of aviation at a time when the nation and the world were struggling to find a way out of the Great Depression. Re-elected, President Roosevelt continued his New Deal programs, gaining more power from the Congress than any president in history. Thousands of young men were put to work in CCC camps building roads, parks, planting forests.

Hitler was also putting his unemployed youth to work in a different manner as was the military leadership of Japan. *Life* magazine devoted articles to German and Japanese youth in military training. John took special interest in a picture of a training device in Germany. It showed a student sitting on a platform above a moving roll of paper upon which was painted overhead views of cities. The German student looked at the moving scene below through a sighting device. John realized he was being taught bombing techniques.

There was a seven-page article on a Chinese warlord who controlled the entire northeast of China. His name was Mao Tse-tung. In the West, his growing Communist army was viewed with curiosity.

In Spain bombs were falling on civilians as John had seen them fall in Ethiopia. Russian planes flown by the leftist republic government of Spain and German planes flown by the rightist rebels sometimes bombed the same city. These raids, beginning with Guernica, were the first mass air attacks deliberately committed against noncombatant civilians in Europe. John had seen it happen first in Ethiopia.

The tanks and planes of Germany would be used as John had seen the Italians use them. He was sure of it. But there were other problems here at home in 1937 to occupy American minds. Unemployment was still the number one problem. Erskine Caldwell's play *Tobacco Road* was breaking all records on Broadway with its depiction of a desperately poor family. That year saw the country's most disastrous flood. The Ohio and Mississippi rivers forced nearly a million refugees in eight affected states to flee their homes. Like many pilots, John volunteered to fly supplies to the flooded areas.

The year John spent successfully promoting his flying school was a disastrous one for America's struggling airlines. In one terrible month five planes and forty-five lives were lost. 1937 was the year that Howard Hughes broke his own transcontinental flight record in a plane that would set design trends in fighter aircraft through the end of World War II.

There was talk of "mystery rays" that could "see" ships and planes miles away, even in the fog. (Articles also talked of x-rays being used against cancer, the "unknown enemy.)"

John, the instructor, was also ever the student, noting changes in technology and aviation as well as in the rapidly changing world around him. He wanted to be a part of those changes and he wanted to give other blacks the skills to be part of it. But was there time?

John had never been blind to the problems of segregation and prejudice. In his home state, one politician, who was Mississippi's present senator and formerly the state's governor, had always used racial fear to get elected. He was so powerful that the phrase "you better see 'the man'" was known to mean Senator Bilbo. John thought it ironic that the word "bilbo" in the dictionary was defined as "a long iron bar or bolt with sliding shackles and a lock, formerly used to confine the feet of prisoners." John had seen the same kind of man in the North but, like Booker T. Washington, he believed the best way to help the advancement of his people was first to teach them the knowledge and skills that were in demand. He was certain that war was coming, and that men with flying skills, white or black, would be needed. Yet he found that even in his own school, he was teaching more whites than blacks. He felt he was not accomplishing enough alone.

But John was not alone. Unknown to him there were others and among them was a fresh graduate of West Point, class of 1936. His name was Benjamin O. Davis, Jr. His father Benjamin O. Davis, Sr., the first Negro to be promoted to the rank of general in the United States armed services, was in command of an all-black cavalry division. (The armed forces at the time were segregated.)

Ben Jr. wanted to fly. He applied for flight training and was refused by a letter signed by the Chief of Staff stating flatly that no Negroes were in the air corps and there weren't going to be any. The young Benjamin decided to keep trying.

Another serious young black flyer was C. Alfred Anderson. He had saved his money and bought a sixty-five hp Veely monocoupe. Because there was no instructor available, he had taught himself to fly.

On one occasion Anderson made a forced landing in a field where he sustained a nasty head injury. Afterwards he had to hide his plane because his mother started carrying an ax and searching the countryside for it. She said if she found the plane she would destroy it to keep her crazy son from killing himself.

Anderson later met a Dr. Forsythe who had originally come from the West Indies. Graduating from Tuskegee, he had gone on to medical school in Canada. He talked Anderson into making a goodwill flight with him to the West Indies. They bought a new monocoupe of ninety hp and named it "The Spirit of Booker T. Washington." Not only did they fly it to the West Indies, they went on to South America, island hopping all the way. They made the flight when Pan American Airways was still pioneering routes to South America with flying boats.

Then in 1939, a former corporal named Hitler invaded Poland. (It seems strange how much trouble former corporals have caused in the world. Napoleon, Mussolini, and Hitler all were discharged from their first try at military duty at the rank of corporal.) President Roosevelt realized he must find a way to greatly increase the number of pilots in the United States. Politically he wanted a way to do it without alarming the country, and especially the voters, with war fright.

The answer was the Civilian Pilot Training Program. Airport operators, badly in need of business, and colleges all over the country applied for the program.

It was not easy for black schools to gain access to the Civilian Pilot Program. Cornelius Coffey who had left

Robinson to start his own flight school was at first turned down when he applied for the program. Tuskegee also was turned down. Coffey flew to Washington to seek help from then Senator Harry Truman. Truman expressed an attitude that was typical of the time. He stated that he didn't believe Negroes could learn to fly. Later, as Vice President, Truman reversed himself and supported training for blacks. He couldn't deny that blacks were capable of flying because, after all, those who came to petition him for the program had flown themselves to Washington. Tuskegee finally received a government grant and by 1940 the college was ready to establish its own aeronautics program.

Thirty-seven year old John Robinson was informed by school officials of Tuskegee's incipient flight program. He received the news with joy, but sadly he decided that he could not be a direct part of the Tuskegee aeronautics school for which he had worked so long. He had obligations to the employees and students of his own school in Chicago. There was something else, too—he had maintained contact with the government of Ethiopia in exile. There was hope that Britain, now engaged in war, would drive the Italians from Ethiopia. John had volunteered his services should the emperor need him.

The man selected to head the flying school at Tuskegee was C. Alfred Anderson. He was assigned two initial tasks. The first was to pick up a new Waco UP-F 7 bi-plane from the factory at Troy, Ohio. The second was to fly it to Chicago for aerobatic training and CAA (Civil Aviation Administration) certification as a flight instructor. During his several weeks' visit in Chicago, Anderson was the guest of Colonel John Robinson who insisted that Anderson stay at his apartment during his training.

The following fall, "Chief" Anderson (as he is fondly called to this day), set up Tuskegee's flying school on a small strip on the Union Springs Highway. A short time later the school purchased land for a new field they named in honor of Dr. Moton, a former president of the school. (In 1986, Anderson was awarded the prestigious Brewer Trophy, given for extraordinary contributions to aerospace education).

By 1941 the war in Europe was raging. Only England remained unoccupied, standing alone against Hitler at a terrible price. The United States air corps was establishing new training bases as quickly as possible. Judge William Hastie, an aide to the Secretary of War, fought, begged, and fought some more for the establishment of a particular army air training base. He finally got it. Judge Hastie was black and the base was built at Tuskegee, Alabama, in July of 1941 for the purpose of training Negro combat pilots.

The air corps sent Lieutenant Colonel Parrish to Tuskegee as director of operations. Col. Parrish, (later promoted to general,) was assigned the task of turning young black men into fighter pilots. Many members of the air corps did not give Parrish very good odds for success when they heard of his task, but he was determined that his command would be no joke.

Shortly after his arrival at Tuskegee, he was visited by a black pilot. General Parrish remembered the brief encounter. "John Robinson conveyed to me how proud he was to see the new program at Tuskegee. I was very favorably impressed by his quiet, sincere manner. He offered to help in any way we might need him." Parrish had no doubt of Robinson's ability. Robinson set an example, and Parrish got on with his assignment.

Eight months later Benjamin Davis, Jr., graduated with four other pilots from the Advanced Flying School at Tuskegee. By the end of the war, more than six hundred pilots graduated from the school. Davis became commander of the first all-black air unit in United States history, the 99th Pursuit Squadron. Equipped with P-40s, the 99th engaged in combat in North Africa in 1943 as part of the 79th Pursuit Group, half of whom were Southern white pilots. It turned out that these men didn't mind what color their wingmen might be as long as they could fly like hell and shoot straight. There was good camaraderie in the 79th. The unit later took part in the invasion of Sicily. In 1944, Davis was given command of the 332nd Fighter Squadron, which he trained in the United States and then took to the Italian theatre of war where his pilots were baptized into combat during the Anzio operation. They flew P-51s, all of which had red painted tails. The troops on the Anzio beachhead saw the "Red Tails" shoot down sixteen German planes in the month of February, 1944. On the 200 escort missions the group flew during the war, not a single bomber was lost. In the closing months of the war, the Germans introduced the Me 262 jet fighter. Lieutenant Roscoe C. Brown of the 332nd Red Tails was among the first pilots in history to engage and successfully shoot down a jet fighter.

Of the six hundred pilots to graduate from the Advanced Flight School at Tuskegee, eighty-three won Distinguished Flying Crosses. Ben Davis, Jr., became the first black general in the United States Air Corps. Another graduate, General Daniel James, Jr., became the first four-star black officer in United States history when he was appointed Commander in Chief, NORAD, Aerospace Defense Command.

# The Emperor Calls Again

In 1943 the British drove the Italian Army from Ethiopia. Shortly thereafter a mysterious "Mr. Strong" left England. His real name was Haile Selassie. The Lion of Judah had prevailed. The British secretly returned the triumphant Selassie to Addis Ababa.

What he found on his arrival devastated him. The Italians had virtually killed off every educated or technically skilled Ethiopian. It would take a generation or more to replace them.

One of the few educators to survive was Mrs. Mignon Inniss Ford who had moved to Ethiopia in 1931 from the United States. She had opened the Princess Zanabe School, the only private school in the country. During the Italian occupation she hid in the outskirts of Addis Ababa helping support her small children by making clothes. Her family had been close friends with the emperor. She first met John Robinson during the war, in the hospital in Addis Ababa where he was recovering from the wounds he had received in combat.

Haile Selassie placed the highest emphasis on schools and lines of communication throughout his country after the war. Mrs. Ford helped reopen the schools. To reestablish the lines of communication in Ethiopia, Haile Selassie once again looked to John Robinson. The emperor determined that Ethiopia must become an essentially air-minded nation. The terrain demanded it. The land was so rugged that modern roads were too expensive to build. Coffee crops could take four weeks by donkey to reach the railroad station in Addis Ababa for shipment to markets outside Ethiopia. By air the same coffee would take only hours to transport. Ethiopia needed John Robinson.

In 1944, at the emperor's request, John Robinson once again settled his business and personal affairs in the United States and left for Ethiopia.

By the time the United States had entered World War II John had been considered too old to fly in the U.S. Air Force. However, at the war department's request he had toured air bases in 1940 and 1941 to discuss his combat experiences in Ethiopia, especially the effectiveness of strategic formation bombing.

Now John Robinson's new task was to build an air force for Ethiopia and to help guide the founding of an Ethiopian airline.

He selected a small group of black pilot instructors as well as airframe and engine mechanics, from the United States to go with him. Ethiopia borrowed $324,089 to fund the new operation. Robinson purchased, borrowed and perhaps liberated enough light training planes to begin building a new air corps for Ethiopia.

Even though the pilot training program grew, the process was too slow to fulfill Ethiopia's immediate air transport needs. In 1946 an agreement was made with TWA Airlines to furnish technical personnel and aircrews to fly a fleet of twelve DC-3 and courier aircraft for Ethiopian Airlines.

After this agreement, John turned his full attention to training Ethiopia's small new air force.

In order to accelerate the rebuilding of his country, Haile Selassie arranged for scholarship programs at U.S. colleges for Ethiopian students. He needed someone to help prepare these students for the cultural shock they would experience when they left Ethiopia for the first time to travel to the most modern country in the world. The task fell to an old friend of John's: Janet Waterford (Bragg) who became known as "Mom" to hundreds of Ethiopian students, who usually arrived in the United States with notes to her from John Robinson. Years later, she recalled, the notes from Johnny often had grease smudges on them, the mark of the ever busy "hands on" aviation instructor, head of "the air force or not".

John lived for a while in a suite at the Netsa Hotel in Addis Ababa, then he was given a beautiful white villa overlooking the airport. (Ironically, it had been built by the occupying Italians.)

John was busy, he was flying, he was happy. He personally taught Prince Makonnen, Duke of Harar, to fly. They became the best of friends, often flying together. He also gave lessons to Mrs. Inniss Ford's son Yosef Ford. (Today Ford lives in Washington and is a professor of anthropology at the Center for Ethiopia.)

Despite John's happiness and success an incident occurred in 1948 which brought home the reality of prejudice and politics, even for an admired and loved black man living in a black-run country.

During the Italian war Count Von Rosen, a Swede, volunteered a plane for use by Ethiopia's ambulance corps. He often flew it himself but it was eventually destroyed in a bombing raid.

After the war Count Von Rosen set a flight record by flying a Swedish Sapphire single-engine training plane from Sweden to Ethiopia. Upon his arrival he was commissioned a major in the new Ethiopian Air Force.

The count let it be known in Addis Ababa's diplomatic community that he was not pleased to be outranked by Colonel Robinson and under his command. Perhaps his blue blood was rebelling against taking orders from any black man below the rank of emperor.

Despite this incident of racism Robinson persevered in building up Ethiopia's Air Force. Through Robinson's efforts the Ethiopian Air Force obtained a surplus American C47 (DC3) cargo aircraft. The C47, which normally requires two pilots as air crew, had to be delivered to Addis Ababa. John and Von Rosen were the most qualified pilots for the job. They both arrived at the pick-up point in separate aircraft. According to witnesses, Von Rosen refused Robinson's order to fly in the right seat as copilot, saying something to the effect that he, Von Rosen "Won't fly with a nigger."

Robinson climbed into the C47 and by himself, flew the large plane to Addis Ababa.

When Von Rosen landed a short while later in a small plane, a few more words were exchanged between the two men and they began fighting. Robinson broke Von Rosen's jaw and, evidently, the pride of Sweden. Von Rosen made a formal complaint and Robinson found himself placed under house arrest for two days. He was visited by Mrs. Ford, Professor Talbart, and other friends who reported that John was very angry.

The emperor's aides later explained that Von Rosen represented Sweden which was at the time furnishing a great deal of support to Ethiopia in the form of supplies, including arms, aviation parts and technical assistance. Von Rosen threatened to have his country's aid terminated. Ethiopia could simply not afford to lose any aid from any source.

Robinson subsequently left the Ethiopian Air Force and joined Prince Makonnen in an import business. He also accepted a royal appointment to head the duke's new aviation school. John and the duke grew to be inseparable friends. The incident with Von Rosen became history and life for John was good.

Then one day in March 1954, in the fifty-first winter of John's life, a call came in requesting an emergency air lift of whole blood to an outlying airstrip for a young man who had been injured by an aircraft propeller.

Robinson quickly volunteered. Bianchi Bruno, an Italian engineer whom Robinson had taught to fly, asked to fly as copilot.

Those who venture into the sky know that there can be circumstances that lead into harm's way, and sometimes all a pilot's skill, knowledge and judgment are not enough.

On the thirteenth of March 1954, a fractured valve destroyed an engine at a critical moment. There was a flaming crash near Addis Ababa. Bruno died in the wreckage. No one knows how John Robinson managed to pull himself from the twisted cockpit and crawl out of the flames.

For two weeks he struggled to live. Addis Ababa came to his aid, the staff of the American Embassy donated blood to him, an emperor stood by him in the hospital, but the Brown Condor would spread his wings no more.

His funeral cortege stretched for miles through the city. Thousands gathered along the way to say farewell to this airman they knew and loved.

Ten thousand miles away, a small, proud, heartbroken black woman clutched a telegram and cried with the pain only a mother can feel. With her small hands she smoothed the wrinkles from the crumpled yellow page and with trembling fingers, placed it in a thick, worn scrapbook. She closed the book, held it close to her, and wept softly.

Somewhere in the writings of another lost airman, Antoine De Saint-Exupéry, the Frenchman tells of his thoughts of flight and death, and a friend he called "Mermez."

> The landscape was still laved in golden sunlight, but already something was evaporating out of it. I know nothing, nothing in the world, equal to the wonder of nightfall in the air.
>
> Those who have been enthralled by the witchery of flying will know what I mean—those who fly professionally and have sacrificed much to their craft. Mermez said once, "It's worth it, it's worth the final smashup."

And so it must have been for John Charles Robinson, 1903-1954.